WIT & HUMOUR
from
ANCIENT CHINA
—100 Cartoons by Ding Cong
Bilingual Edition
Translated by Ma Mingtong

NEW WORLD PRESS
BEIJING, CHINA

CONTENTS

Ding Cong and His Cartoons   5
    by Gladys Yang and Yang Xianyi

Cartoons and Ancient Tales   12

List of Titles   212

Ding Cong and His Cartoons

This collection of jokes has been chosen from histories, biographies, novels and anecdotes dating from the 3rd century B.C. to the 17th century. It ridicules stupid officials, pokes fun at pretensions or follies and records smart repartee, displaying much the same style of humour throughout two millennia.

As the Chinese have a strong sense of humour, many such anthologies have been compiled. This one, however, has the outstanding attraction of illustrations by Ding Cong, one of China's most popular and respected artists.

Ding Cong, now sixty-nine, still signs his work Little Ding. He first did so in his teens to distinguish himself from his father Ding Song, a veteran cartoonist in Shanghai. Ding Song's home was frequented by actors, writers and painters, and from his boyhood Little Ding loved art. But an artist's life was so hard in those days that his father did not want him to follow in his steps; he refused to teach him. Art was the youngster's hobby and he learned from life, taking a sketch-book with him wherever he went. His only formal training was a term of drawing classes at the Shanghai Fine Arts Institute.

Like virtually all Chinese artists of his generation Ding Cong has had a very chequered career. The Anti-Japanese War forced him to move from Shanghai to the Interior. Later, Kuomintang's censorship and persecution of radicals drove him from Shanghai to Hong Kong. After Liberation the anti-Rightist movement and the "cultural revolution" robbed him for twenty years of the freedom to publish under his own name. Under these circumstances it is amazing that he has achieved so much. On the other hand, the ups and downs of his life have toughened him, enriched his experience and deepened his sympathy for all underdogs.

Ding Cong started his career by drawing cartoons and helping to edit film magazines and pictorials. In the Interior and Hong Kong he also designed stage sets and costumes — experience which stands him in good stead when illustrating stories from the past. With the outbreak of the Pacific War in 1942 he went back to the Interior and contributed to the exhibition "Hong Kong in Torment." His travels with a repertory company brought him in touch with social outcasts, whose sufferings he often took as his theme. Thus his *The Red Light District* and other drawings of social phenomena portray the hard life of prostitutes in Chengdu as well as the rampant corruption in wartime China. In recognition of his outstanding work he was made a member of the Modern Art Association.

In 1944 he drew brilliant illustrations for Lu Xun's masterpiece *The True Story of Ah Q*, satirizing the landlord and Imitation Foreign Devil but showing sympathy for feckless Ah Q, considering him as a victim of his times. This sympathy for the poor and ignorant pervades all his illustrations.

Returning to Shanghai in 1945, and later when he returned to Hong Kong, Ding Cong drew cartoons attacking the Kuomintang's reactionary regime. "Cartoons can be compared to daggers," he said. "Armed with them I have pierced through dark and gloomy times."

After Liberation Ding Cong came to Beijing, became an editor of the *China Pictorial*, drew cartoons, illustrated stories and helped to design exhibitions. One of our earliest recollections of him is when, like a smiling Buddha, he showed us round the fascinating exhibition of the classical novel *A Dream of Red Mansions* which he had been instrumental in arranging. The wealth of material assembled shed light on the novel and its historical background, the costumes and furnishings of that time, even the tricks resorted to by desperate candidates to cheat in the imperial examinations.... That was one of the best exhibitions we have seen.

In 1957, wrongly labelled as a Rightist, Ding Cong was sent to the Great Northern Waste to work on the land. Though the temperature sometimes dropped to 30 degrees below zero, he never complained but retained his sense of humour. In 1960 he was cleared and given a job in the National Art Gallery. But in 1966 came the "cultural revolution," he was sent to a cadre school and then to the countryside to work as a swineherd.

When rehabilitated in 1979, Ding Cong determined to make up for lost time. His work is in great demand. His cartoons keep appearing in papers and magazines. He has illustrated many books by such famous writers as Lu Xun, Lao She and Mao Dun, as well as many others. After making a careful study of these works he faithfully reflects and illuminates them with his meticulous draftsmanship and his keen sense of character and period.

Ding Cong is an all-round artist but above all a brilliant cartoonist and illustrator. A good illustration should do more than simply reproduce what a writer has said: it should give it a new dimension by adding the artist's insight. This Ding Cong does most successfully, using his cartoonist's eye to select significant details and bring out salient features without drawing caricatures. His illustrations in this book are not merely amusing but forceful and thought-provoking. Over the years he has evolved his distinctive style and simplified his compositions. His drawings can be recognized at a glance. The speed with which he now works is based on painstaking practice.

We once had the privilege of seeing Ding Cong in action. In a friend's home one evening a poet complained that some bureaucrats, to pose as cultured, write up third-rate poems or calligraphy everywhere. Then our hostess brought out a newly made rice paper lamp-shade, and we urged Ding Cong to paint something on it. In five minutes he had produced a smug mandarin in red robe and official hat, proudly flourishing a brush. The poet added the irreverent inscription, "I passed this way and peed here."

Ding Cong's old friends still call him Little Ding, not simply because he won fame under this name but because of his lovable childlike qualities. He is frank, enthusiastic and straightforward, full of fun and with no malice in his make-up. Wherever he goes we hear laughter. "The style is the man" — this applies to both writers and artists.

Ding Cong now advises the literary journal *Du Shu*. One of China's prolific artists, he is working tirelessly to delight the reading public. As he says, "I am nearly seventy and must make the most of my time."

Gladys Yang and Yang Xianyi
July 1985

丁聪和他的漫画

这个插图本笑话集是从公元前三世纪到公元十七世纪的一些笔记小说和历史传记中选出的，内容是对某些昏庸官僚和装模作样的愚蠢人的讽刺小品，包括一些机智的对话，反映了近两千年间中国人民的古老幽默。

中国人民是很富于幽默感的，历代曾有过许多这样的笑话选集，但这本选集的插图是出自当代中国最受欢迎的一位美术家丁聪之手，因此而大大增色。

丁聪现年六十九岁，但他还自称为"小丁"。他的父亲丁悚是过去上海的一位漫画家。丁聪在十几岁时就随他父亲作画。他的家中经常有一些著名戏曲演员、作家和美术家作客，因此他从小就喜爱艺术。当时一个画家的生活是很艰苦的；他的父亲并不想鼓励他成为画家，也不愿意教他画画；他开始只是拿绘画当作业余爱好。他开始只作一些生活速写。后来也只在上海美专正规学习了一个学期。

同他一代的大多数画家一样，丁聪经过一个颠沛流离的生活。抗日战争迫使他离开上海去到内地，后来由于国民党对文艺的审查制度和政治迫害，他又被迫流亡香港。解放后的反右运动和"文化大革命"又剥夺了他二十年的创作自由，不能发表许多署自己名字的作品。即使这样，他还能生产大量的作品，这是很令人惊异的。艰苦生活环境磨炼了他的意志，丰富了他的生活经验，也使他对过去受苦受难的老百姓增加了感情。

丁聪开始创作主要是搞漫画，同时也编辑过电影画报，作美术编辑工作。在内地和香港期间还设计过舞台布景。这些经验对他为小说作插图都有帮助。一九四二年太平洋战争开始时，他从香港回到内地参加"香港受难"展览。他还随剧团到各地写生，接触到当时难民生活，画出他们困苦的处境。如他在成都曾为当时妓女的悲惨生活画了一幅"花街"，还画了其它揭露战时国民党腐败社会的画面。由于他的贡献，他当时就是中国美术家协会的一位杰出代表。

在一九四四年，他为鲁迅的名著《阿Q正传》画了插图，讽刺了当时的地主阶级和假洋鬼子，对天真的阿Q的苦难遭遇表示了同情。他当时的插图大都反映了他对贫苦大众的深厚感情。

一九四五年他回到上海，后来又去到香港。他当时画了不少抨击国民党反动统治的漫画。他曾经说过："漫画有如匕首，可以用来刺穿那个黑暗悲惨的年代！"

解放后，他来到北京，编辑了《人民画报》，又画了不少漫画和书籍插图，设计过各种展览。还记得，当他在五十年代初为古典小说《红楼梦》设计一次历史背景展览时，他总是笑咪咪地，象弥勒佛那样，兴致勃勃地带着我们看他的各种美术设计。那次展览中大量的资料提供了《红楼梦》一书的历史背景，当时的服装和生活用具，甚至包括应考的学员在考场作弊时所带的夹带材料等等。那是我们所见过的最有趣味的一次展览。

一九五七年丁聪被错划右派，被送到北大荒劳改。虽然有时气温低到零下三十度，他毫无怨恨情绪，还保持着他的幽默。一九六〇年他恢复名誉，到美术馆工作，但在一九六六年又发生了"文化大革命"，又被送到干校，在农村养猪。

一九七九年他恢复自由，决定要补上所失掉的时间。 许多方面都请他作画，他的许多漫画在许多报纸和刊物上发表，他为许多著名作家如鲁迅、老舍和茅盾等等的小说画了插图。在认真研究这些作品之后，他精心绘制了插图，忠实地反映了作品内容、人物性格和时代。

丁聪是一位多才多艺、技巧全面的画家，特别擅长的是漫画和书籍插图。一幅好的插图不仅要能反映出作家所说的内容，而且要能加深作品的艺术深度。丁聪正是成功地做到了这一方面。他以画家敏锐的洞察力选出重要的细节，取其精华，而不使人物漫画化。他为这本书所做的插图不仅使人觉得有趣，而且使人深思。他的独特风格和简洁手法是长期探索的果实。他的速写使人一看就懂，他作画速度惊人，往往一挥而就，而这正是他苦心经营的成绩。

我们曾有一次机会看到丁聪作画。一天晚上，在一位朋友家里，在座的一位诗人谈起有些官僚冒充风雅，喜欢在名胜地方乱涂乱写。后来这家主人拿出一个新制的纸台灯罩，请丁聪在灯罩上画几笔，他只用了几分钟的时间就画出了一个身穿红袍、头戴纱帽的官僚，手里拿着毛笔。那位诗人就为这个画题上"到此一游"并比之为到处撒尿。

丁聪的老朋友们都叫他"小丁"，这不仅是因为他年少成名，而且是因为他"不失其赤子之心"，为人非常坦率真诚正直。他到哪里，人们都可以听到他爽朗的笑声。他的作品的风格正反映了他本人的性格。

丁聪现在是《读书》杂志的美术顾问。他不知疲倦地经常发表新作品，产量惊人。他自己常说，他快到古稀之年了，必须加倍努力。

戴乃迭　杨宪益
一九八五年七月

11

1. Talent in Childhood

When he was only ten years old, Kong Rong of the state of Eastern Han went to visit a noted scholar named Li Ying. The boy demonstrated his talents before Li and his guests by properly answering a number of questions put to him.

The boy was praised by all the guests present except one. The majority was of the opinion that if the boy was so clever at the age of ten he would have a promising future.

A man named Chen Wei expressed a different view: "If one is too clever in childhood he will be unlikely to make any great achievements when he grows up."

Kong Rong replied: "On the basis of what you have just said, it is clear that you were a very clever child."

小 时 了 了

东汉孔融，十岁时，去见当时的大学者李膺。宾客很多，他有问必答，显出才能。

客人都加以夸赞，说小时候这么聪敏，将来一定大有作为。

有个名叫陈炜的，持有不同意见，他说："小时候过于聪敏懂事，长大了未必有什么了不起。"

孔融接口便说："听您这么说，想来您小时候一定很聪敏懂事了！"

2. Zhuge Ke

Zhuge Liang, of Three Kingdoms fame, had an elder brother named Zhuge Jin, who was otherwise styled Zhuge Ziyu. The latter had a long face, so people nicknamed him "Donkey Face". He worked under Sun Quan, the ruler of the state of Eastern Wu. Zhuge Jin had a son named Zhuge Ke. Diligent in his studies and naturally clever, the boy was praised as a prodigy.

One day Sun Quan was holding a grand feast for his ministers. He ordered a man to bring in a donkey. A piece of paper with the words "Zhuge Ziyu" on it was attached to the donkey's face, implying that Zhuge Jin had a face as long as a donkey's. This caused everyone present to break out laughing and caused Zhuge Jin great embarrassment.

At this difficult moment, Zhuge Ke knelt before Sun Quan and asked his permission to add two words to what was already written on the paper. Sun Quan agreed.

Zhuge Ke wrote "donkey of" before his father's name, thereby changing the original derogatory meaning.

The ruler had no way of preventing the donkey from being dragged away by Zhuge Ke free of charge.

诸 葛 恪

诸葛亮有个哥哥诸葛瑾，字子瑜，因面孔长得长，有人称他为驴脸。他在东吴孙权手下当差。他有个儿子叫诸葛恪，因勤奋好学，又聪敏，当时被誉为神童。一日，孙权大宴群臣，叫人牵来一头驴，用纸写了"诸葛子瑜"四个字，贴在驴面上，意思是：诸葛瑾的脸长，象驴脸，惹得在场的人哄堂大笑，使诸葛瑾很难堪！

诸葛恪马上跪到孙权面前，要求用笔添两字。孙权说："好吧。"

诸葛恪就在"诸葛子瑜"下面添了两个字"之驴"。你再看："诸葛子瑜之驴。"

孙权毫无办法，只能让他白白拉走一头驴。

3. Deer or River Deer

Wang Pang, the son of Wang Anshi (a noted scholar and official of the Song Dynasty) was playing at a friend's house, where there was a deer and a river deer in a cage.

The master of the house asked Wang Pang: "Can you tell which of the animals is a deer and which is a river deer?"

Wan Pang, who was less than ten years old, was unable to distinguish the two. But he said: "The one next to the river deer is a deer, and the one next to the deer is a river deer."

是 獐 是 鹿

王安石的儿子王雱，到人家去玩。

这人家有个笼子，笼子里有一只獐、一只鹿。

主人问王雱，哪只是獐，哪只是鹿。

王雱才几岁，分辨不出獐和鹿来，当时便答道："獐旁边的是鹿，鹿旁边的是獐。"

4. The Man Who Lost Himself

A runner not noted for his intelligence in a government office was assigned to escort a convicted monk . Before departing he made a careful check of everything he needed to bring along on the trip, and wrote the following list: "Parcel, umbrella, cangue, official document, monk, myself." Along the way he kept reminding himself of the items on the list.

The monk was aware of the runner's stupidity, and plied him with wine until he got drunk. He then cut off all the runner's hair and put the cangue around his neck before his escape.

When he recovered from his intoxication, the runner said to himself: "Let me check my list now." He found the parcel and umbrella. Then felt the cangue around his neck and said: "Yes, the cangue is here. And here's official document." Finally he said in surprise: "Oh, the monk has disappeared!"

But when he touched his bald head, he said with relief, "I'm glad the monk is here. But how can I locate myself?"

我 不 见 了

一 呆役解罪僧赴府，临行恐忘记事物，细加查点，又自己编成两句曰："包裹雨伞枷，文书和尚我。"

途中步步熟记此二句。僧知其呆，用酒灌醉，剃其发以枷套之，潜逃而去。

役酒醒曰："且待我查一查看，包裹雨伞有。"摸颈上曰："枷，有。"见文书，曰："有。"忽惊曰："哎呀，和尚不见了。"

顷之，摸自光头曰："喜得和尚还在，我却不见了。"

5. Six Legs Are Quicker Than Four

A government office issued an urgent document to be distributed among its subsidiary organs. To ensure that it be delivered in time, the messenger was provided with a horse.

Running behind the horse, the messenger whipped the horse until it was galloping at full speed. Someone asked him in amazement: "If it's such an urgent mission why don't you ride the horse?" The messenger answered: "Running on six legs is certainly quicker than four, isn't it?"

下　公　文

有个官府，要紧急地下达公文，怕送得迟了，就给送公文的拨了一匹马。那人赶着马走，有人问他道："这么紧急的事情，你为什么不骑马？"

那人答道："六只脚走，难道不比四只脚走得快吗？"

6. Reporting a Poor Harvest

Once an old farmer went to the district magistrate to report a poor harvest. The magistrate: "You mean that there was no yield at all?"

The farmer: "The wheat yield was thirty percent, the cotton yield twenty percent, and the rice crop yielded a little more than twenty percent."

After making a rough calculating, the magistrate became angry and shouted: "That means a seventy or eighty percent yield. How can you call that a poor harvest?"

The farmer: "For the 140 or I50 years, I have never experienced such a serious crop failure."

The magistrate: "Are you really 140 or 150 years old?"

The farmer: "I am seventy years old, my first son is over forty, and my youngest is over thirty. That's a total of 140 or 150 years."

报 荒 年

老农民到县里报灾荒。

县官问："庄稼一点收成都没有吗？"

回道："麦子只收三成，棉花只收二成，稻子只收二成多。"

县官一算，生了气，喝道："一共收了七八成，还报什么荒！"

农民道："我活了一百四五十岁，实在没有见过这样重灾。"

县官说："你有一百四五十岁吗？"

农民回道："我七十岁，大儿子四十几岁，小儿子三十几岁，一共不是一百四五十岁吗！"

7. Personal Security

Sun Yan'gao, a prefectural governor, was besieged by an army of Turks. He was so scared that he remained indoors and was too scared to go to office. The issuing and acceptance of official documents had to be handled through a window.

When he learned that the attackers were approaching his mansions he locked the door and hid in a closet. At the last minute, he told his servant: "Take good care of the key. When the enemy gets here, make sure you don't give it to them."

呆 刺 史

刺史孙彦高，被突厥围城，不敢出厅视事，征发文符，俱于小窗接入。及报贼登垒，乃锁州宅门，身入柜中，令奴曰："牢掌钥匙，贼来慎勿与。"

8. The Ridiculous Magistrate Assistant

Ma Xin, a native of Shandong, was the magistrate assistant of the Changzhou district. One day he took a boat to visit his superior. His superior asked: "Where is the boat berthed?"

"In the river." replied the assistant.

The enraged superior scolded him loudly: "What a sack of straw!"*

Ma Xin answered immediately: "The sack of straw is on the boat."

---

* Meaning an idiot or a fool.

呆 县 丞

有个长洲县丞名唤马信，山东人。有一天坐着船去拜见上官，上官问道："船停在什么地方？"

"船在河里。"

上官大怒，大声责骂道："真是大草包！"

马信立即应声道："草包也在船里。"

9. A Man of Phlegmatic Temperament

A man of phlegmatic temperament was sitting with a friend beside a stove. When he noticed that the hem of the friend's robe was burning, he said hesitantly: "I have just noticed something. If I tell you about it now, I am afraid you may become impetuous. But if on the other hand I don't tell you, it may cause you a serious loss. Shall I tell you or should I remain silent?"

The friend asked him what the problem was. After a pause, the man said slowly: "Your gown is on fire!"

The friend hurriedly snuffed out the fire, and said angrily: "Since you know my robe was on fire, why didn't you tell me earlier?"

The man continued speaking in his unhurried manner: "I first thought you might be an impetuous person. Now I know it is true."

慢 性 子 人

有个慢性子的人和朋友一同围着炉子烤火，看见朋友的衣裳角被烧着了，他却慢吞吞地说："有件事情，我已经早就看见了，想说吧，怕你性急；不说吧，又怕你损失太大，你看，我到底是说好呢？还是不说好呢？"

朋友问他什么事。这人寻思了半天，才又慢慢地说："是你的衣裳烧着了！"

朋友急忙起来，把火弄灭，愤怒地说："你既然早就发现了，为啥不早说呢！"

这人仍慢条斯理地回答："我说你是个急性子嘛，果然一点不错。"

10. The Daughter-in-Law's Glib Tongue

Once upon a time there was a daughter-in-law who had a glib tongue. One day at lunch time she served a bowl of rice to her father-in-law.

After tasting the first mouthful, the old man remarked with satisfaction: "The rice today is very tasty. I would like to have three bowls of it."

Upon hearing the old man's words of praise the daughter-in-law said: "Yes, I cooked the rice."

But when the father-in-law took the second mouthful, he became annoyed and said: "Ouch, there's a stone in it!" The daughter-in-law then said: "My sister-in-law washed the rice."

The old man then stirred the rice with his chopsticks and sniffed at it. "Why, this rice is burnt."

"My mother-in-law was in charge of the fuel." she replied.

巧 嘴 媳 妇

从前，有一个巧嘴媳妇，煮好了米饭，先盛给公爹一碗。

公爹吃了一口就称赞道："今天的饭很香，我可要吃三大碗。"

巧媳妇听了公爹的夸奖，忙说："嘻，这顿饭是我做的。"

于是公爹又开始吃第二口，可饭刚送到嘴里就听见"咔嚓"一声，公爹立刻叫道："哎呀，这么多的砂子！"

巧媳妇忙说："那是小姑淘的米。"

公爹把筷子在饭里搅了两下，闻了闻，问道："怎么，这饭还有点糊味？"

巧媳妇这次回答得更干脆："那是妈烧的火！"

11. A Bargain

Two men planned to distil wine together. One of them said: "You provide the rice and I'll supply the water." The other man said: "If all the rice comes from me, how should we divide the distilled wine?" The first man: "There will definitely be no cheating. When the wine is ready I only want the water back. The rest goes to you."

合 做 酒

甲乙谋合本做酒。甲谓乙曰:"汝出米,我出水。"乙曰:"米都是我的,如何算账?"甲曰:"我决不欺心,到酒熟时,只还我这些水便了,其余都是你的。"

12. The Top Hat

Flattery is referred to as "placing a top hat" on someone's head. Two disciples appointed to their first official posts went to see their tutor. The latter told them: "In this world, following the proper path will do you no good. It is better if you place top hats on other people's heads."

One of the disciples said: "You are right. Most people in this world like wearing top hats. You, however, are an exception." The tutor was very much pleased with this comment.

Upon leaving, this disciple said to his companion: "I've just given away my first top hat."

高 帽 子

世俗谓媚人为顶高帽子。尝有门生两人，初放外任，同谒老师者，老师谓："今世直道不行，逢人送顶高帽子，斯可矣。"其一人曰："老师之言不谬，今之世不喜高帽如老师者有几人哉！"老师大喜。

既出，顾同谒者曰："高帽已送去一顶矣。"

13. A Face Painted Red

There once was a man whose daily life was constrained by numerous taboos. At joyous celebrations the colour red played a prominent role in all the decorations in his home.

When a guest arrived riding a white horse, the animal was not allowed to enter the stable. Another guest, who was well aware of the man's habits, appeared with face painted red to offer his congratulations.

The host was very much surprised, but the well-wisher explained: "I know that you do not approve of the colour white. Thus I dare not appear before you with my plain white countenance."

Note: White is the traditional colour for mourning and death in China. Red is used on happier occasions.

红　脸

有个人多所忌讳，家里有喜庆事，一切都要带红色。客人骑着白马来，被赶出门，不让进到马房。另一个客人就涂个大红脸，登堂道贺。主人惊讶。这个客人解释道："知道老先生不喜欢素的，所以不敢用白脸前来。"

14. Wisdom in a Single Finger

Once upon a time there was a Daoist fortune-teller. So great was his ability that people came from near and far to seek out his services.

One day three scholars about to sit for the imperial examinations in Beijing came to enquire about which of them would be the successful candidate. The trio lit sacrificial incense sticks and kowtowed before him.

With his eyes closed, the priest pointed his index finger at them in silence. The scholars could not understand this gesture and asked the priest for an explanation.

The Daoist priest picked up his elk-tail whisk and said: "The Divine Will cannot be disclosed." The trio went away rather disappointed.

After their departure, a young disciple asked the priest: "Master, which of the three scholars will be successful?" The priest: "The exact number is already known."

"Does a single finger mean that only one will be successful?"

" Yes."

"But what if two of them are successful?"

"Then it means one of the three will fail."

"And what if all three of them are successful?"

"A single finger implies that all will pass at one time."

"And if all of them fail to pass the examinations?"

"My single finger means that not even one of them will be successful."

The disciple quickly saw the point and said: "So this is the Divine Will!"

"一" 的 妙 用

据说，从前有个道士专会给人算命，算得十分灵验，前往找他算命的人很多。一天，有三个要进京赶考的考生，想问问三人当中谁能考中，就到道士那里说明来意，点了香、叩了头。只见道士闭着眼朝他们伸出一个指头，却不说话。考生们不明其意，求道士说明。道士拿起拂尘一挥，说道："去罢，到时自然明白，此乃天机，不可言明。"三个考生只好快快地走了。

考生们走后，小道童好奇地走过来问道："师父，他们三人到底有几个得中？"

道士说："中几个都说到了。"

"你这一个指头是什么意思？是一个中？"道士说："对。"

道童说："他们要是中了两个呢？"道士说："这就是有一个不中。"

"那么他们三个要是都中了呢？""这一个指头就是一齐中。"

"要是三个都不中呢？""这就叫一齐不中。"

小道童恍然大悟地说："原来这就是'天机'呀！"

15. Cursive Calligraphy

Prime Minister Zhang was fond of excessively cursive calligraphy and ignored the way other people ridiculed his handwriting.

One day he wrote a poem in his typical style and ordered his nephew to copy it in standard script. Though the boy was generally accustomed to his way of writing, he failed to identify some of the characters and had to ask the prime minister.

When the official looked at his writing again, he too was unable to identify them. So he became angry and scolded the youngster by saying: "Why didn't you come to me earlier?"

草　字

张丞相喜欢写草字，常常出格，别人笑他，他全然不管。有一天，他做了一首诗，飞笔写了，却叫侄儿给誊抄下来。

侄儿虽然看惯了他的字，但还有认不得的，只好去问他。

他端详了半天，自己也认不出来。这时他发脾气了，责备侄儿说："为什么不早问呢？"

16. The General's Unworthy Belly

Dang Jin, a general of the Song Dynasty, was rude and entirely devoid of wisdom. Yet he was fortunate to hold a high official position and was served sumptuous meals every day.

One day after dinner he patted his belly and said outloud: "I have never been unfair to you."

A man standing next to him who had a clever tongue said: "You have never been unfair to your belly, but your belly is indeed unworthy since it has never provided you with any ideas!"

Later, people called Dang Jin "the General with an Unworthy Belly."

Note: The belly rather than the mind is regarded in China as the source of wisdom.

腹 负 将 军

党进是宋朝一位将军,粗鲁没有智谋,只是官运亨通,高居一品。他吃的全是山珍海馐。

这天,吃完了饭,拍拍肚皮说:"我没有对不起你啊!"

旁边有个快嘴的人,当时接口说:"将军没有对不起肚皮,可是肚皮很对不起将军,因为他从来没有给将军出过一点主意啊!"

后来人就称这种将军为"腹负将军"。

17. No Wine in an Old Bottle

There was once a rich man who had a reputation as a skinflint. One day he sent his servant to buy wine, handing him a bottle but no money. The servant asked: "Master, how can I possibly purchase wine without any money?"

The miser replied angrily: "Anyone can buy things with money. It takes a wise man to obtain wine without paying for it."

The servant then went away with the bottle, and soon came back with it still empty. He said to his master: "Here is the wine."

The niggardly old man was so enraged when he discovered an empty bottle before him that he cursed his servant: "This is really outrageous! The bottle is empty. What shall I drink?"

The servant replied: "Anyone can drink if there is wine in the bottle. You are indeed a capable man if you can get wine out of an empty bottle."

打 酒

从前有个财主，是个刻薄鬼。有一次刻薄鬼叫仆人去买酒，只给仆人一只酒瓶，却不给钱。仆人感到莫名其妙，便问："老爷，没有钱怎么能买到酒呢？"

刻薄鬼生气地说："花钱买酒谁不会？不花钱买到酒，才算有能耐呢！"

仆人听了，便拿着瓶走出去。过了一会儿，仆人又拿着空瓶回来说："酒买来了，请喝吧。"财主一见是空瓶，大发雷霆地骂道："真是岂有此理！酒瓶里没有酒，叫我喝什么？"

仆人答道："酒瓶里有酒谁不会喝？要是能够从空瓶里喝出酒来，才算真有能耐呢。"

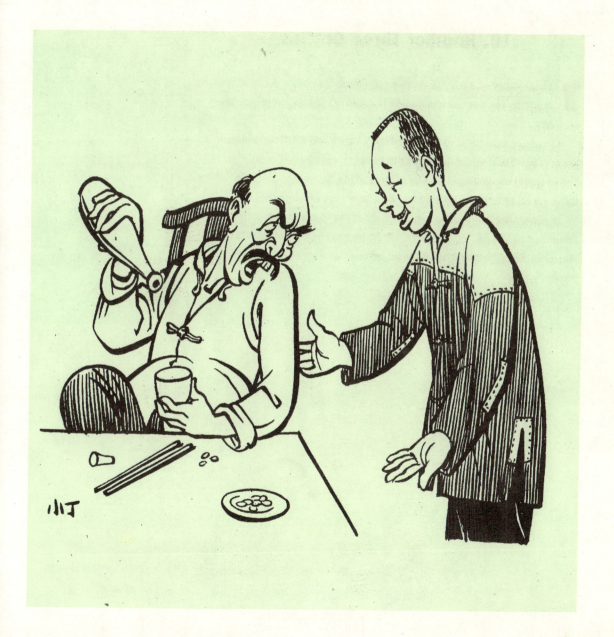

18. Another Three Catties

The stupidity of a certain district magistrate was often the source of laughter. He was a drunkard and finished off several catties of wine each day.

One day a man came to the magistrate's office and made an oral complaint. The official sat for the hearing in an angry mood, as the man's unexpected arrival was getting in the way of his drinking. So without going through the usual procedures, he ordered that the complainant be flogged.

A runner knelt down and, requiring about the number of strokes to be administered, asked: "How many?" As he had not recovered from his inebriation, the magistrate raised three fingers and said: "Another three catties, please."

再 打 三 斤

某县令甚呆，所为多可笑，其纰缪不可枚举。饮量甚洪，日必沽数斤，怡然独酌。一日，突有喊冤者，正醺醺时，阻其雅兴，含怒升堂，拍案喝打，并不掷签，役跪请曰："打若干？"官伸指曰："再打三斤。"

19. Yearning for the Third Year

On taking up his post, a new official asked his subordinate: "How should an official act?" His subordinate replied: "Act honestly in the first year, act in a semi-upright way in the second year, and just muddle along in the third year." The official sighed: "How can I hold out until the third year?"

如 何 熬 得 到 第 三 年

新官赴任，问吏胥曰："做官事体当如何？"吏曰："一年要清，二年半清廉，三年便混。"官叹曰："教我如何熬得到三年！"

20. Poor Memory

A member of the Imperial Academy was known for his poor memory. One day he invited some guests for lunch. The invitations had been delivered in good time, and a feast was being prepared in the kitchen.

On the day of the event, however, the scholar forgot all about it, and went instead to the home of one of those who had been invited. They chatted till lunchtime, when the friend had no choice but to ask the scholar to stay for lunch.

The scholar's relatives sent a man to find him, but the scholar only stared the man in the face and said: "Why have you come here? If you urge my friend to leave who will be my host at lunch?"

健　　忘

一位翰林公，是个健忘的人。一天他请朋友吃午饭，已经下了请帖，厨房备了酒菜。到了当天，他却忘了，反而去他所请的朋友家里，山南海北地谈天。临到午饭的时候，也不说走，这个朋友只好留他吃饭。翰林公的家人，照老规矩到时候来催客。他瞪眼说："你是哪家派来的？你把请我的主人请走，我到哪里吃饭呢？"

21. Neither Salt Nor Vinegar

Lu Mai was in the habit of taking neither salt nor vinegar. A friend asked him: "How can you stand it without salt or vinegar in your food?"

Lu retorted: "How can you stand it eating both salt and vinegar every day?"

不　吃　盐　醋

卢迈不吃盐醋。

朋友问他:"您每天不吃盐醋,怎么受得了呢?"

卢迈反问道:"您每天都吃盐醋,又怎么受得了呢?"

22. A Lost Black Gown

Cheng Zi of the Song Dynasty once lost a black gown and couldn't find it anywhere.

One day on the street he noticed a woman clad in a black dress and began to follow her. Puzzled by his behaviour, the woman queried: "What do you want?"

Cheng Zi answered: "I have lost my black gown."

"What do I have to do with your black gown?"

"Let me have your black dress."

"But it's mine."

Cheng Zi continued with grievances: "What I have lost is a silk lined gown, while your dress is a simple unlined garment of cotton. I shall certainly get the worst of this bargain. Isn't it to your benefit to give it to me?"

黑 色 衣 服

宋国的澄子先生，丢了一件黑色衣服，四处去寻找。

在马路上，遇见了一个穿黑衣服的妇人，他就跟在后面，紧盯着不放。

妇人问："你要干什么？"

澄子先生说："我丢了一件黑衣服。"

"你丢了黑衣服，与我什么相干？"

"就用你这一件赔我吧！"

"这是我自己的呀！"

澄子先生很委屈地说，"我丢的是一件绸的黑夹衣，你这一件是布的黑单褂。用你的布的黑单褂，抵我的绸的黑夹衣，我很吃亏了，你有什么划不来呢！"

23. Bargain over a Corpse

A rich man of the state of Zheng was drowned in a Weihe River flood and his body was salvaged by a fisherman. When the members of the rich man's family came forward to claim the body, the fisherman asked for a large amount of gold as a reward. Not knowing what to do, they approached Deng Xi for advice.

Deng said: "Remain calm and wait! No one else will come forward to claim the corpse." And so they followed his advice.

The fisherman became impatient, since he could not keep the body for very long. So he too went to Deng Xi for advice.

Deng told him: "Wait a while and don't worry. You're the only person they can get the corpse from."

尸 首 买 卖

洧河忽然发大水，淹死了郑国一个财主。

财主的尸首被人打捞起来。

财主家里前来赎买尸首，打捞的人索取很多黄金做报酬。财主家里去找邓析先生讨个主意。

邓析先生说："别着急，等等！ 他除了卖给你家，哪能卖给别人哩！"

财主家里果然不去买了，打捞的人，不能把尸首老放着，有些急了，也去找邓析先生讨个主意。

邓析先生说："别着急，等等！ 他除了在你这里买，别处哪能买得到哩！"

24. Happy Fish

Zhuang Zi and Hui Zi were strolling along the Haoshui River. Observing the swimming fish, Zhuang Zi said: "Look how freely the fish are swimming about. They must be very happy."

Hui Zi said: "You are not a fish. How do you know that they are happy?"

Zhuang Zi added: "You are not I. How do you know that I do not know the happiness of the fish?"

鱼　　乐

庄子和惠子同游，来到濠水上，看见水里白鲦鱼游来游去，庄子说："白鲦鱼悠游自在，多么快乐呀！"

惠子说："您也不是鱼，怎么知道鱼的快乐呢？"

庄子说："您也不是我，怎么知道我不知鱼的快乐呢？"

25. A Knock Means No Knock

Master Shan of the Song Dynasty was a noted monk who maintained close ties with official organs. Qiu Jun, a minor official, came to the temple one day to see the monk, but he sat unmoved, ignoring his visitor completely and affecting an air of snobbishness.

A while later, the son of a high military official arrived. Master Shan hurriedly stood up, bowed and welcomed the caller.

Qiu Jun was rather embarrassed. After the young caller left, he queried the monk: "Why do you treat your visitors differently?"

The monk replied with a Buddhist formula: "Reception means non-reception, while non-reception means reception."

On hearing this, Qiu Jun raised his walking stick and struck the monk on his bald head.

The monk, trying to avoid a further beating, said: "Why are you, a faithful Buddhist, behaving in this manner?"

Qiu Jun said: "In my case, a knock means no knock, but no knock means a knock."

打 是 不 打

宋朝有个和尚叫珊禅师，和官府交通往来，是个有名气的和尚。

丘浚是个小官，这天来到庙里，请见珊禅师。珊禅师坐着不动，爱理不理，非常傲慢。

坐了一会，有个大军官的子弟来了。珊禅师听到知客僧通报，慌忙起身，降阶相迎。

丘浚心里很不舒服，等那大将军的子弟走了，就质问珊禅师："为何待客礼数不一样？"

珊禅师打着禅语回答道："接是不接，不接是接。"

丘浚闻言，举起手杖，劈头劈脑向珊禅师打去。

珊禅师一面闪躲，一面说："施主为何如此？"

丘浚说："我打是不打，不打是打。"

26. An Indicator of Age

The groove at the median line on one's upper lip is called the philtrum. One day, at a grand feast with his ministers, Emperor Wu Di of the Han Dynasty said: "A book of physiognomy says that if a man's philtrum measures one inch long he will live to be one hundred years old."

Dongfang Shuo, who was present, was convulsed in laughter.

The emperor said: "Did you laugh because what I said lacks common sense?" Dongfang Shuo answered: "I am not taking Your Majesty as a source of ridicule. I'm thinking about Peng Zu. It is said that Peng Zu lived to be eight hundred years old. If the book of physiognomy is correct, Peng Zu's philtrum must have been eight inches long. What a long face he must have had!"

人 中 主 寿

人鼻子下面，嘴唇上面那个微微凹下的部位，名叫"人中"。
汉武帝有一天在大会群臣的时候，忽然提出："看相的书上说，人中如果有一寸长，就可以活到一百岁。"

东方朔在一旁哈哈大笑。

汉武帝说："你笑寡人说得没有常识么？"

东方朔回答道："臣不敢笑陛下，臣只笑那个彭祖。人们都说彭祖活到八百岁，如果照看相书上所说，他的人中有八寸长，只不知他的那张脸够多么长！"

27. An Excessive Ban

The state of Shu, one of the noted Three Kingdoms, once placed a ban on wine distilling, resulting in many brewers being sent to jail. Even those who had idle stills in their homes were arrested. Some believed this excessive measure would make life impossible for the people of Shu. Liu Bei, the ruler of the state, ignored this opinion.

One day, when Liu Bei was out riding with Jian Yong, they saw a man in the distance. Jian said: "Have this man arrested immediately as he is likely to commit a criminal offence!"

Liu Bei asked: "How do you know that?"

Jian Yong said: "This man has an organ growing on his body which may be an accessory to a rape."

Liu Bei burst into laughter and realized the necessity of setting free of those people who had been arrested for having idle stills in their homes.

随 身 工 具

蜀国严厉禁酒。把那些酿酒的人，都抓起来问罪。甚至有些人家，从前藏有酿酒工具，被查出来，也同样处罚。有人认为不可以，刘备只是不听。

这天，简雍随刘备出游，远远看见路上一个男人走过，简雍说："把他抓住，这是个强奸犯人！"

刘备问："你怎么知道的？"

简雍说："这人随身带有强奸工具呀！"

刘备哈哈一笑，就命令把那些家藏酿酒工具的人放了。

28. A "Bright" Idea Solves a Matrimonial Dilemma

The daughter of a man of the state of Qi was the object of courting by two young men. Her eastern neighbour was ugly but came from a wealthy family, while her western neighbour was handsome but poor.

Finding this problem insoluable, the girl's parents put the matter straight before her. The girl's solution was to extend a favourable positive answer to both parties.

When queried as to how she could realize her plan, the girl said: "I'll take my meals at the house of my eastern neighbour but reside at that of my western neighbour."

如　意

齐人有女，二家同往求之，东家子丑而富，西家子好而贫，父母不能决，使其女偏袒示意。女便两袒，母问其故，答曰："欲东家食而西家宿。"

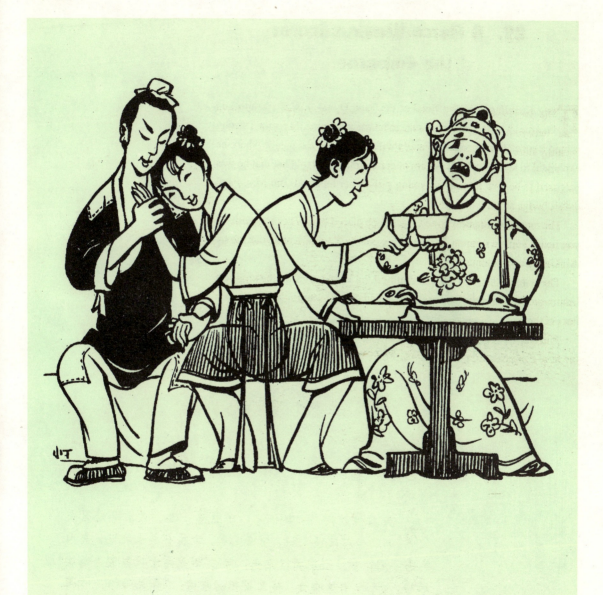

29. A Fierce Woman Scares
the Emperor

Fang Xuanling, a high official of the Tang Dynasty, was a henpecked husband who lacked the courage to take a concubine. Emperor Taizong issued a special order to have Fang's wife brought to the palace where he explained to her the official system of concubinage and told her that he was prepared to bestow a beautiful young girl on her husband. But Mrs. Fang didn't budge an inch.

The emperor ordered a wine vessel to be placed before her and said: "If you insist, you are running counter to my orders. You must end your life by drinking this poisonous wine."

The wife of the high official emptied the vessel without the slightest hesitation. But since the emperor had only intended to intimidate her, it was not poisonous.

The emperor remarked later: "If she scared me like this, can you imagine how Fang Xuanling feels?"

帝　怕　妒　妇

房夫人性妒悍，玄龄惧之，不敢置一妾。太宗命后召夫人，告以媵妾之流，今有定制，帝将有美女之赐。夫人执意不迴，帝遣斟卮酒以恐之，曰："若然，是抗旨矣，当饮此鸩。"夫人一举而尽，略无留难。帝曰："我见尚怕，何况于玄龄？"

30. Choosing a Wife

A resident of the state of Chu had two wives. Another man tried to seduce the two women in order to take advantage of their husband. First he tried his tricks on the elder one, but was treated with a thorough swearing. Next he approached the younger one, who finally fell prey to his entreaties.

Before very long, the husband of the two women died. Both of them were prepared to marry again.

After some preliminary questioning, the go-between asked the interloper: "Which of the two women do you wish to marry?"

"I prefer the elder one."

The matchmaker replied: "Didn't the elder woman curse you? And didn't the younger one comply with your wishes? Why do you prefer the elder one?"

"What you say is true. As long as she was another man's wife, I was glad to have her become my lover, but I prefer a fierce woman who knows how to swear and is unlikely to become another man's lover."

挑 选 老 婆

楚国有个人，有两个老婆。

另外有个人，想诱惑她两个。先勾引年纪大些的，挨了一顿臭骂；后勾引年纪小些的，却接受了求爱。

过了不多久，两个老婆的男人死了，两个老婆都预备改嫁。

有人从中说合，问那个人："你愿意娶那个年纪大些的、还是愿意娶那个年纪小些的？"

"我愿意娶那个年纪大些的。"

"那个年纪大的不是詈骂过你吗？那个年纪小的不是接受过你求爱吗？为什么你倒要挑选那个年纪大的呢？"

"是这样：在别人家里，我希望她接受我求爱，做我的情妇；在我自己家里，我却希望她能詈骂人，不做别人的情妇。"

31. Seven Pairs of Earrings

The king of the state of Qi was about to remarry after the death of his first empress. A wise man suggested to Prime Minister Xue that he would be rendering a useful service if he could recommend a suitable woman to the monarch.

The prime minister said: "Originally I had the same idea. The emperor has seven concubines who are all very close to him, but it's impossible to determine which is the emperor's favourite. If my recommendation differs from the emperor's choice I would certainly offend the new empress."

The wise man said: "If you want to discover the emperor's favourite, present the emperor with seven pairs of earrings. Six pairs should be identical in quality and style, but the seventh pair should be of much higher quality. When you learn which of the seven concubines receives the best earrings, you will understand the emperor's thinking on the subject."

Xue took his advice. When the emperor chose his new empress, she was the same woman recommended by the prime minister.

七 付 耳 环

齐国王后死了，还没有立新王后。

有人向丞相薛公说："您趁此机会，建议国王，选个王后，不是有功吗？"

薛公说："我原有此意。只因国王有七位妃子，都很亲近，也不知道国王最中意谁，如果弄差了，国王选中的和我举荐的不一样，那我就要得罪新王后了。"

"您要知道国王最中意的是谁，那好办。您可以向国王献上七付耳环，其中六付是普通的，一色一样，另外一付却是特别精美好看的，过一天，您看哪位妃子戴着这精美的耳环，不就明白国王的心事吗？"

薛公听得这话有理，就照着办。后来齐国立了王后，果然恰是薛公举荐的。

32. Saving a Minister's Life

After the death of the emperor of Qin his empress became the head of state. Her illicit relationship with a minister named Wei Choufu was no longer a secret in court circles.

A number of years later, the empress fell ill and knew that her days were numbered. She prepared her will in which she stated that after her death Wei Choufu would be buried alive with her.

On learning this Wei naturally was greatly perturbed and sought advice from another minister named Rong Rui. When Rong held an audience with the empress, he asked her: "Do you think people still have feelings after death?"

"No, the dead cannot have feelings."

"If that is so, why sacrifice your favourite minister? If the emperor or his soul had any feelings all those years he's been waiting six feet under, then you should hurry up and apologize for your long absence. What's the use of bringing Wei Choufu along to see him?"

The empress accepted this argument and revoked her will.

殉　　葬

秦国老王死了，皇后执政，人称"宣太后"。

宣太后爱着一个臣子，名叫魏丑夫，朝野咸知，也不是什么秘密。

过了些年，宣太后生病，自己觉得不行了，就下了一道遗嘱，说是我死之后，一定得用魏丑夫殉葬。

殉葬等于活埋。魏丑夫得到消息，十分惊恐，就去找大臣庸芮，设法解救。

庸芮进宫见太后，开言问道，"你以为人死之后还有知觉吗？"宣太后说："没有知觉了。"

"你既然以为人死无知，为什么用您生前所喜爱的人去殉葬一个无知的死人呢？死者若是有知，老王在地下发脾气已经有些日子了，您表示歉意还来不及，带了魏丑夫去能够伺候您甚么呢？"太后说："对！"就取消了那个遗嘱。

33. Unacceptable Quotations

The wife of a physician named Yang was known for her jealousy.
One day Yang began repeating some poems in the "Zhou-Nan" chapters of the *Book of Songs*:

"Like *jiumu* (a tree with branches growing downward), the empress treated her subjects with a kind heart and without jealousy."

"Only when there is no jealousy, may proper relations prevail between husband and wife."

"In the absence of jealousy there will be many children in the family."

When his wife asked him the name of the book, the physician said: "The *Book of Songs*."

"Who is the author?"

"Duke of Zhou."

"No wonder. If it were written by his wife, she would have never said any of this."

妇 人 嫉 妒

杨郎中妻赵氏，性嫉妒。一日，杨郎中只管把毛诗周南数篇反复读之，云："樛木，后妃逮下也，言能逮下而无嫉妒之心焉。"又云："不妒忌，则男女以正。"又云："不妒忌，则子孙众多也。"其妻问其甚书，答曰："毛诗。"问："甚人做？"答曰："周公做。"其妻云："怪得是周公做，若是周婆做时，断不如此说也。"

34. Cutting Out the Arrow Shaft

Once a soldier who had an arrow stuck into his flesh went to consult the docter.

The surgeon cut off the arrow shaft and said: "That is all. You may go now."

The soldier said: "But the arrow head is still deep in my flesh!"

Shaking his head, the surgeon said: "That's a matter for an internist. The surgical part of the operation is finished."

Note: In contrast to internal medicine, surgery in Chinese medicine is known as "external medicine."

剪 箭 管

有个医生，自称是外科专家。

有一次，一个士兵中箭后从阵地回来，痛得不行，赶忙请他来医治。

这位医生不慌不忙，拿起并州剪刀，"咔嚓"一声把露在外边的箭管剪掉，说道："好了！"

士兵说："箭头还在肉里哩！"

医生摇摇头说："那是内科的事，我外科的手术已经做完了。"

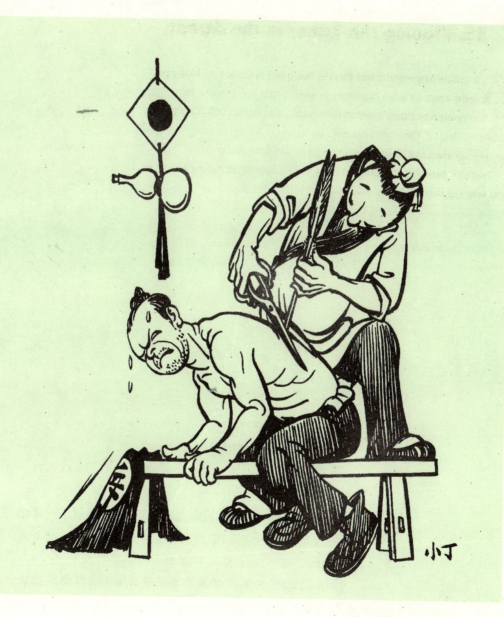

35. Playing the Zither in the Street

An unskilled musician was playing the zither in the street. Many passersby came to listen expecting to enjoy some good music, but gradually dispersed when they realized how poorly he played. Only one person remained behind. Quite pleased with himself, the musician said: "At least one person appreciates my playing."

But the man said: "That's my table your zither is sitting on. I have to take it home eventually; otherwise, I would have left long ago."

市 中 弹 琴

琴师于市中弹琴，市人以为琵琶三弦之类，听者甚多，及闻琴声清淡，皆不喜欢，渐次都散。惟一人不去，琴师喜曰："好了，还有一个知音，也不辜负我了。"

其人曰："若不是这搁琴桌子是我家的，今伺候取去，我也散去多时了。"

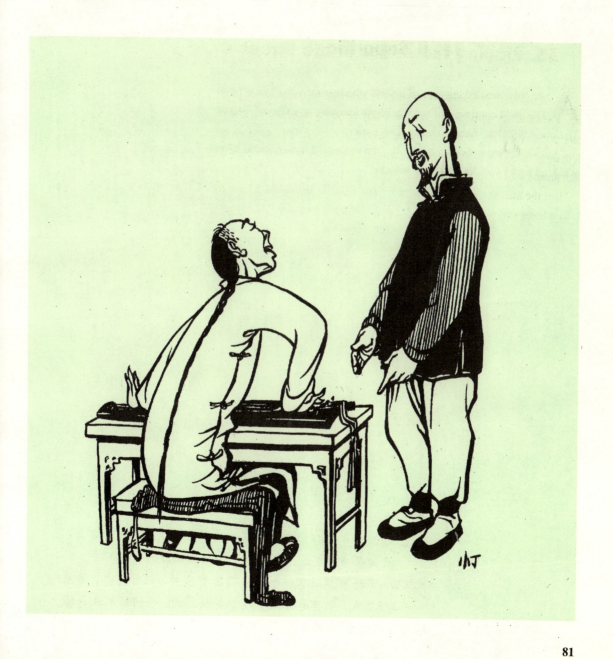

36. A Soporific

A wetnurse was taking care of a child who was the son of an official. The child continued to weep without showing any sign of fatigue. The nurse urged the father to bring her a book.

Answering the official's query, the nurse said: "I have noticed when you read books you often become drowsy."

瞌 睡 法

有一乳母哺养小儿，因儿啼哭不肯安睡，乳母无奈，蓦然叫官人，快拿本书来，官人问其何用，应曰："我每常间见官人一看书便睡着了。"

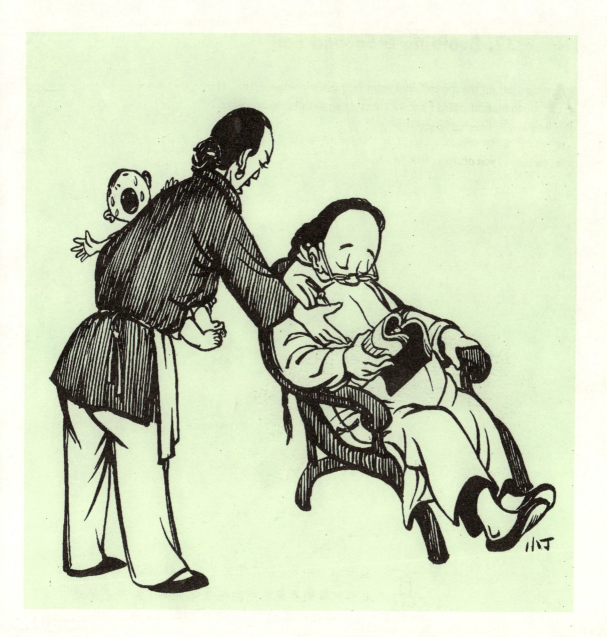

37. Avoiding a Second Fall

A man fell on the ground, and soon fell down a second time. He said to himself: "Had I known I was going to fall a second time, I would have not gotten up so soon."

跌

有个人忽然摔倒在地，刚站起来又摔倒了，于是他道："早知道还有一跌，倒不如干脆不起来也好。"

38. Who Will Look After Me?

The son of a wealthy man was thirty years old, but was such a good-for-nothing that he had to rely on his father for his subsistence. He passed his days in a thoroughly muddleheaded manner.

One day his father, who was then fifty, called in a fortune-teller. The latter predicted that he would die at the age of eighty, and that his son would die at the age of sixty-two.

The son began wailing and said: "My father will only live to eighty. Who will take care of me for the two years after I am sixty?"

谁 养 活 我

有个有钱人的儿子，已经三十岁了，还是什么都不懂，依靠着父亲胡里胡涂地过日子。

一天，他父亲请来算命先生算命。他父亲五十岁了，算命先生给算了一下，说可以活到八十岁。又给他算了一下，说可以活到六十二岁。

他一听就很伤心地哭了起来，说"我父亲只能活到八十岁，那我六十岁以后的两年靠谁来养活呢？"

39. Salted Eggs

Two idiots were eating together. One of them took a salted egg and said in surprise: "I have often eaten eggs, but have always found them tasteless. Why is this one salty?"

His companion answered: "You're fortunate that you have asked a wise person. That salty egg was laid by a salted duck."

腌 蛋

甲和乙都很呆笨。甲偶尔吃了个腌蛋，惊讶地说道："我经常吃的蛋，味道都很淡，不知为什么只有这个蛋是咸的？"

乙说道："我是最聪明的人，亏你问着我。这咸蛋，就是腌鸭子生出来的。"

40. Why Dogs Show No
Respect to Beggars

Once a man asked a beggar: "Why do dogs always bite you?" He answered: "If I were attired in a fine robe I would also be respected by dogs."

Note: The "dogs" in the beggar's answer implies something beyond the four-legged canine creature.

狗　　咬

有个人问叫化子道: "狗为什么看见你们就要咬呢？"
叫化子答道: "我若是有好衣帽穿戴，这狗东西也会敬重我的！"

41. Why People Shiver in Cold Weather

Born in a wealthy family, Huang Xueqian was a fifth-rank official. Yet he was totally unaware of the sufferings of the common people.

On a winter day he was out in the street and saw a beggar shivering. Puzzled, he asked his attendant: "Why is that man shivering?"

The attendant responded: "He is shivering because of the cold weather." The official was even more puzzled and added: "Won't his shivering make him warmer?"

冷　和　抖

黄学乾生长富贵之家，捐了个五品官，只是不知民间疾苦。

冬天，他出外，见到一个乞丐，站在寒风里发抖。他觉得奇怪，就问随从的人："这个人身子怎么老在动弹？"

随从的人告诉他："因为天冷发抖。"

他更觉得奇怪了，说："难道抖抖就不冷了吗？"

42. A Difference of Words

On assuming a new office, a self-proclaimed honest official put up the following notice in his office:

1. I have no desire for money
2. I do not yearn for a higher post
3. I'm not afraid to die

A few days later someone made the following emendations:

1. in small amounts.
2. unless it's higher than this one.
3. but I would like to live as long as possible.

三　不　要

新官上任，自称是清官，不怕丢官，要拼命给百姓做好事，在大堂上贴了标语，上写："不要钱，不要官，不要命。"

过了几天，那张标语下面，却被人逐条加了两个字："不要钱，嫌少；不要官，嫌小；不要命，嫌老。"

43. Exploiting the Earth

When a corrupt official returned home after completing his term of office, he found an old man whom he did not recognize in his home.

When asked who he was, the old man said: "I am the earth of your district."

"Why are you here?"

"Because you exploited the earth."

Note: "Exploiting the earth" means exploiting money.

剥　地　皮

　　一官甚贪，任满归家，见家属中多一老叟，问此是何人。
　　叟曰："某县土地也。"问因何到此，叟曰："那地方上的地皮都被你剥将来，教我如何不随来。"

44. A Pair of Wild Talkers

During the days of the Qin Dynasty two brothers were fond of saying wild things to hoodwink each other.

One day the elder brother said: "Everything we say is totally groundless. Let's go to the brook in front of our house and wash away our nonsense." The younger brother agreed.

The elder brother concealed a piece of ham in his hand and jumped into the water. When he emerged from the water he had a big smile on his face and began to chew on the meat.

His younger brother asked him: "Where did you get the meat?"

The elder brother replied: "The Dragon King was holding a feast and offered me a piece of meat when he learned that I was going to wash away my nonsense. This meat is so delicious it must be a slice of dragon's liver."

The younger brother immediately removed his clothes and dived into the water. But he dived so fast that he smashed his head against a rock. When he came out of the water his head was bleeding profusely.

The elder brother said: "How did you manage to hurt your head?"

The younger brother replied: "The Dragon King was angry because I was late and beat me over the head with a drumstick. The pain is unbearable."

兄 弟 虚 妄

秦时有人家二兄弟，专好妄语，凡有事便相绐。一日，思量云："我二兄弟说话是无凭，可去门前深溪澡浴，洗去妄语。"弟曰："诺。"兄手中先把得一片干脯，脱衣入溪，没水中去，少时出来，着衣服了，歙头摆脑，吃此一片干脯。弟问："何处得肉脯吃？"兄云："海龙王会客作席，见我来洗去妄语，遂得一片与我，滋味甚别，必是龙肝珍味。"其弟闻得，便脱衣，亦钻入水中去，去势稍猛，忽被顽石撞破头，忙出来，鲜血淋漓，兄问："你头如何破著？"答云："龙王嫌我来得迟，将鼓槌打数十下，痛不可忍。"

45. Longing for the Human World

Dong Yong was noted for his filial piety. By order of the Heavenly King, a female immortal was married to him. The parting words of the other immortal maidens were: "Don't forget to send us a message if you find any other men as filial as he."

Note: Legend has it that Dong Yong of the Western Han Dynasty sold himself into slavery in order to pay for his father's burial. His filial act moved the Heavenly King who arranged the marriage.

仙 女 思 凡

董永行孝，上帝命一仙女嫁之。众仙女送行，皆嘱咐曰："此去下方，若更有行孝者，千万寄个信来。"

46. Don't Damage the Tiger's Skin

A man was trapped by a tiger. In an attempt to save him, the man's son took a cutlass and rushed towards the wild beast. At this juncture, the man shouted at the top of his lungs: "My dear son! My dear son! Attack its feet, not its skin, which is worth its weight in silver!"

莫 砍 虎 皮

—— 人被虎衔去，其子要救父，因拿刀去杀虎，这人在虎口里高喊说："我的儿，我的儿，你要砍只砍虎脚，不可砍坏了虎皮，才卖得银子多。"

47. A New Robe

A man was wearing a new silk robe for the first time. Throwing his shoulders back and strutting boldly, he hoped others would notice his outfit. After a while, he asked his attendant: "Are people looking at me?" The attendant replied: "There's no one around." He relaxed his shoulders and said: "Since there's no one here now, I'll take a rest."

夸 新 裙

一人穿新绢裙出行，恐人不见，乃耸肩而行。良久，问童子曰："有人看否？" 曰："此处无人。" 乃驰其肩曰："既无人，我且少歇。"

48. Hot Tea

A peasant from the countryside was in the city visiting a relative, who served him tea made with precious Songluo spring water. The peasant enjoyed the tea so much that he said "Excellent!" over and over, and thus his relative thought he could truly appreciate fine things. He asked his country cousin: "Are you referring to the tea or to the water?" The peasant said: "It's the hotness of the tea which I like the most."

热 得 有 趣

乡下亲家进城探望城里亲家，待以松萝泉水茶，乡人连声赞曰："好好。"亲翁以为彼能识物，因问曰："亲家说好，还是茶叶好，还是水好？"乡人答曰："热得有趣。"

49. Buzi and His New Trousers

Buzi, a native of Zhengxian, asked his wife to make him a new pair of trousers. When he was asked the style of the new trousers, Buzi said: "Just like my old trousers." His wife put a few holes in them so they would resemble the old pair.

卜 子 做 裤

郑县人卜子，使其妻为裤，请式，曰："象故裤。"妻乃毁其新，令如故裤。

50. An Unsuccessful Haircut

A barber was giving a man a haircut, but did a very sloppy job of it. So he stopped cutting and departed, saying: "Your scalp is too tender for haircut. I'll be able to cut your hair properly in a few days when your scalp is strong enough to take the razor."

头 嫩 了

—— 待诏替人剃头，才举手便所伤甚多，乃停刀辞主人曰：
"此头尚嫩，下不得刀，且过几时，姑俟其老，老再剃
罢。"

51. Cooking a Goose

A man noticed a wild goose flying across the sky. He was about to shoot it with an arrow, and said: "Once I shoot it down I shall have it stewed." His brother intervened and said: "A goose flying straight ahead is good for stewing, while one which flies in circles is good for roasting." This squabble continued until they met an old man who advised cutting the goose in half, one half for stewing and the other for roasting. They accepted this suggestion, but when they returned to the original spot the goose was gone.

争 雁

昔人有睹雁翔者，将援弓射之，曰："获则烹。"其弟争曰："舒雁烹宜，翔雁燔宜。"竞斗而讼于社伯。社伯请剖雁烹燔半焉。已而索雁，则凌空远矣。

52. The Pain Next Door

A man suffered greatly from pain in his foot. He told his servant: "Dig a hole in the wall," and then put his foot through the hole into his neighbour's courtyard. Asked why he did this, he said: "If my foot hurts in my neighbour's yard, no longer has anything to do with me."

让 他 去 邻 家 痛

里中有病脚疮者，痛不可忍，谓家人曰："尔为我凿壁为穴。"穴成，伸脚穴中，入邻家尺许。家人曰："此何意?"答曰："凭他去邻家痛，无与我事。"

53. A Felt Hat

One hot summer day a man was seen in the street wearing a warm felt hat. He took a rest under a tree and fanned himself with the hat to cool himself. He said to himself: "If I didn't have this hat, I would have died of the heat."

热　死　我

有暑月戴毡帽而行路者，遇大树下歇凉，即将毡帽当扇，曰："今日若无此帽，就热死我。"

54. Stealing a Pair of Shoes

Zheng Renkai, former magistrate of Mizhou Prefecture, was a corrupt official. When his servant reminded him that he needed to purchase a new pair of shoes, he ordered a subordinate who was wearing new shoes to climb a tree and pick fruit for him. He then ordered his servant to steal the shoes the subordinate had left on the ground. The latter complained bitterly to the magistrate, who retorted: "It's not my job to look after your shoes."

刺 史 偷 鞋

郑仁凯性贪秽，尝为密州刺史。家奴告以鞋敝，即呼吏新鞋者，令之上树摘果，俾奴窃其鞋而去。吏诉之，仁凯曰："刺史不是守鞋人。"

55. No Difference in Price

Feng Dao and He Ning were colleagues in a government office. One day He Ning asked Feng Dao: "I see you bought a pair of new shoes. How much did they cost?" Feng raised his left foot and said: "Nine hundred cash." He Ning became upset, and reproached his servant with these words: "How did you manage to spend 1,800 cash for my shoes?" Feng then lifted his right foot and said: "But this one cost 900 cash too."

一 靴 九 百

冯道、和凝同在中书，一日，和问冯曰："公靴新买，其值几何?" 冯举左足曰："九百。" 和性褊急，顾吏诟责曰："吾靴何用一千八百?" 冯举右足曰："此亦九百。"

56. An Empty Abdomen

A scholar failed several times at the imperial examinations. His wife, who had suffered from intense labour pains during childbirth, said to him: "Succeeding at the examinations is as difficult as childbirth." The scholar's reply was: "At least you had something in your abdomen, but mine is empty."

Note: An empty abdomen is a term implying a lack of knowledge.

肚 里 没 有

一士屡科不利，其妻素患难产，谓夫曰："中这一节，与生产一般艰难。"士曰："你却是有在肚里，我却无在肚里。"

57. Chewing Sugarcane

A man was chewing on some shreds of sugarcane which another man had spit onto the ground. It was of course tasteless, and he said angrily: "What a greedy devil. He has obviously enjoyed himself to the utmost."

嚼 甘 蔗 渣

—— 人拾甘蔗渣而嚼之，恨其无味，乃骂曰："哪个馋牢，吃的这等尽情。"

58. Talking to a Golden Arhat

A man unearthed a golden Arhat. He patted the head of the sculpture and asked it: "Where are the other seventeen of you?"

Note : Arhat is a respected Buddhist sage. According to Buddhist legend, there are eighteen Arhats altogether.

问 金 罗 汉

有掘地得金罗汉一尊者，乃以手凿其头不已，问："那十七尊何在？"

59. The Death of a Lazy Woman

A lazy woman was totally dependent on her husband for her meals. One day, her husband was about to leave home on a trip for four or five days, and afraid that his wife might die of starvation, baked her a pancake large enough to last her for five days, which he fastened around her neck. On his return, however, he found that his wife had died of starvation three days before. On closer examination he discovered that she had only eaten that portion of the pancake which was directly in front of her mouth, and had left the rest of the cake untouched.

懒　　妇

——妇人极懒，日用饮食，皆丈夫操作，她只知衣来伸手，饭来张口而已。一日，夫将远行，五日方回，恐其懒作挨饿，乃烙一大饼，套在妇人项上，为五日之需，乃放心出门而去。及夫归，已饿死三日矣。丈夫骇，进房一看，项上饼只将面前近口之处吃了一缺，饼依然未动也。

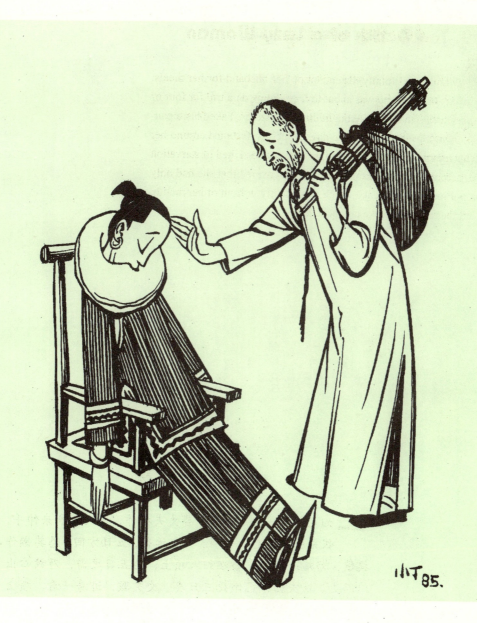

60. The Missing Leg

In the countryside in the old days, people sat on simple stools with legs made out of tree branches. In one house, one of the legs of a stool was broken, and the master sent his servant into the hills to find some suitable material to replace it. The servant left with an axe and returned at the end of the day empty-handed. Answering his master's reproach, the servant said: "There were plenty of tree branches, but none of them were growing downwards."

觅 凳 脚

乡间坐凳，多以现成树丫叉为脚者。一脚偶坏，主人命仆往山中觅取。仆持斧出，竟日空回，主人责之，答曰："丫叉尽有，都是朝上生，没有向下生的。"

61. Walking in the Rain

A man was walking slowly in the rain when someone asked him why he wasn't walking faster. He answered: "It's raining up ahead as well."

徐 行 雨 中

有徐行雨中者，人或迟之，答曰："前途亦雨。"

62. A Fart

A number of people were sitting together when one of them farted. They all grew suspicious of a person sitting with them and started saying nasty things about him. The innocent man laughed out loud without making the slightest protest. Asked why he was laughing, the man said: "The man who farted is among those resorting to abuse."

骂 放 屁

群坐之中有放屁者，不知为谁，众共疑一人，相与指而骂之，其人实未放屁，乃不辩而笑，众曰："有何可笑?"其人曰："我好笑那放屁的也跟在里头骂我。"

63. Ignorance

By mistake a man put on a pair of boots with soles of different thicknesses. He felt uncomfortable and asked himself: "Has one of my legs grown longer than the other? Or is the road uneven?" A passerby told him: "Your boots have different sized soles." So he sent his attendant home to fetch the proper boot. After a long while, the attendant returned empty-handed and said: "The boots you have at home also have different sized soles."

恍　惚

一人错穿靴子，一只底儿厚，一只底儿薄，走路一脚高，一脚低，甚不合适。其人诧异曰："今日我的腿，因何一长一短？想是道路不平之故。"或告之曰："足下想是穿错了靴子。"忙令人回家去取。家人去了良久，空手而回，谓主人曰："不必换了，家里那两只也是一厚一薄。"

64. Painting the Back of One's Head

A stingy man asked a painter to paint a portrait of himself, and offered him a total of three cash for the paper, ink and artist's fee. So the painter used coarse paper and drew the back of the man's head. The man was surprised and asked the artist: "A portrait should show a person's countenance. Why have you drawn the back of my head?" The artist's reply was: "My advice to a person as stingy as you is not to show your face to others."

画 行 乐

——人极鄙啬,请画师要写行乐图,连纸墨谢仪共与银三分。画师乃用墨笔于荆川纸上画一反背像。其人惊问曰:"写真全在容貌,如何反背呢?"画师曰:"你这等省银子,我劝你莫把脸面见人罢。"

65. How to Get Rich Quick

An immortal with the ability to turn rocks into gold was dispatched to the human world to test people's greed with an end to recruiting new immortals. But he was having a lot of trouble finding the people, since in all cases the persons he chose were dissatisfied with the size of the pieces of gold he was offering them. Finally, the immortal came across a man who refused his generous offer, which he presented as follows: "When I point at this stone with my finger, it will turn into gold, and you may have it."

The immortal thought that the man felt that the rock was not big enough, so he pointed at a bigger piece. "I will point at this big piece and turn it into gold for you." But the man shook his head again. The immortal took this as an indication that he was entirely devoid of greed. Having decided to invite him to become an immortal, he asked him: "You appear not to want gold. What is it you want after all?"

The man said: "All I want is to transplant your fingers onto my hand. In this way I too can turn rocks into gold and gain endless wealth."

愿 换 手 指

有一神仙到人间，点石成金，试验人心，寻个贪财少的，就度他成仙，遍地没有，虽指大石变金，只嫌微小。末后遇一人，仙指石谓曰："我将此石，点金与你用罢。"其人摇头不要。仙意以为嫌小，又指一大石曰："我将此极大的石，点金与你用罢。"其人也摇头不要。仙翁心想，此人贪财之心全无，可为难得，就当度他成仙，因问曰："你大小金都不要，却要甚么？"其人伸出手指曰："我别样总不要，只要老神仙方才点石成金的这个指头，换在我的手指上，任随我到处点金，用个不计其数。"

66. Beijing Beating Me Better

A youngster back from a visit to Beijing boasted of the quality of everything in the capital. One night he was walking with his father in the moonlight. A passerby said: "The moon looks very nice tonight." The youngster intervened and said: "How can you say that? The moon in Beijing looks even nicer."

His father scolded him with these words: "There is only one moon in the sky. How can you say that the moon in Beijing looks nicer!" The father struck his son with his fist. His son shouted in tears: "Being beaten is rarely a good thing, but getting beaten in Beijing is better than this."

拳 头 好 得 狠

有一人自北京回家，一言一动，无不夸说北京之好。一晚偶于月下与父同行，路有一人曰："今夜好月。"夸嘴者说："这月有何好，不知北京的月好得更狠。"其父怒骂曰："天下总是一个月，何以北京的月独好？"照脸一拳打去。其子被打，带哭声喊曰："希罕你这拳头，不知那北京的拳头好得更狠。"

67. Revenge

An unworthy son showed disrespect to his father, while the man took especially good care of his grandson. A neighbour asked him: "Your son is not filial, yet you devote so much of your time to your grandson. Why?" He answered: "My aim is to bring up my grandson to give vent to my anger and take revenge on his father when he grows up."

出　　气

一不肖子常殴其父，父抱孙不离手，甚爱惜之。邻人问曰："令郎不孝，你却甚爱令孙，何也?"答曰："不为别的，我要抱他长大了，好替我出气。"

68. A Guest's Witty Remark

A guest was sitting in the courtyard waiting for dinner. Suddenly the host stole into the dining room and started tasting the dishes on the table. At this juncture, the guest said in a loud voice: "This is a lovely dining room, but what a pity that the beams and columns have been damaged by worms."

The host rushed out and asked: "Where are the worms?" The guest replied: "They are eating inside the beams and columns, how can I tell you where they are?"

背 客 吃 饭

有客在外，而主人潜入吃饭者，客大声曰："好一座厅堂，可惜许多梁柱都蛀坏了。"主人忙出曰："在哪里？"客曰："他在里面吃，外面如何知道？"

69. The Emperor's Crown and Robe

Back from Beijing, a beggar boasted that he had seen the emperor. Someone asked him: "What was the emperor wearing?" The beggar said: "He had on a carved white jade crown and a robe made of pure gold." The man replied: "How can the emperor bow with his hands clasped if he is wearing a golden robe?" The beggar scoffed at the man and said: "You are indeed an idiot. The emperor doesn't have to bow to anyone."

皇 帝 衣 帽

乞丐从北京回来，自夸曾看见皇帝。或问："皇帝如何装束？"丐曰："头戴白玉雕成的帽子，身穿黄金打成的袍服。"人问："金子打的袍服，穿了如何作揖？"丐啐曰："你真是个不知世事的，既做了皇帝，还同那个作揖？"

70. A Fondness for Drinking

A father and his son were carrying a vat of wine on a carrying pole. The road was slippery and they broke the vat. The father became very angry, but his son lay down on the ground and started to drink the spilled wine. Raising his head, the youngster asked his father: "What are you waiting for, some cooked dishes to accompany the wine?"

好　　酒

父子扛酒一坛，路滑打碎。其父大怒。其子伏地大饮，抬头向父曰："难道你还要等菜？"

71. Perpetual Drowsiness

The deputy magistrate of Huating went to visit a local gentleman. As the latter failed to appear for some time, the visitor became drowsy and fell asleep in a chair in the sitting room. Before long, the gentleman appeared, but when he discovered the magistrate sleeping he was reluctant to wake him up. So he sat down opposite to him and fell asleep. The gentleman and the official woke up and fell asleep in turn for the rest of the day. Finally the magistrate left without disturbing the gentleman who retired to his private chamber when he awoke.

好　　　睡

华亭丞谒乡绅，见其未出，座上鼾睡。顷之，主人至，见客睡，不忍惊，对座亦睡。俄而丞醒，见主人熟睡，则又睡。主人醒，见客尚睡，则又睡。及丞再醒，暮矣，主人竟未觉，丞潜出。主人醒，不见客，亦入户。

72. Tailoring Official Gowns

During the reign of Emperor Jiajing of the Ming Dynasty, a Beijing tailor became famous for his fine work and a prominent official called him in to tailor an official robe. The tailor knelt down and inquired about the official's title and length of service. After the official expressed his surprise, the tailor explained: "When an official assumes a high post for the first time, he will throw out his chest in high spirits and he will lean slightly backwards, thus the front of his robe must be a little longer than the rear. For the official midway through his career, who feels settled, the front and rear parts of his robe must be of equal length. When an old experienced official wishes to change his position or is ready to retire, he will bend a bit. In that case, the front part of his robe will be shorter than the rear part. Without knowing your title and length of service, it will be impossible to cut a suit to fit you properly."

裁　　　缝

嘉靖中，京师缝人某姓者，擅名一时，所制长短宽窄，无不称身。尝有御史令裁员领，跪请入台年资。御史曰："制衣何用知此？"曰："相公辈初任雄职，意高气盛，其体微仰，衣当后短前长；在事将半，意气微平，衣当前后如一；及任久欲迁，内存中抱，其容俯，衣当前短后长；不知年资不能称也。"

73. Moving the Sacred Images

In a certain temple a clay image of Laozi stood to the left of image of Buddha. Looking at the positions of the two images, a Buddhist monk said: "Our Buddha's doctrine is extensive and profound. Why is he seated on the right?" He then reversed the positions.

Later, a Taoist priest noticed that the positions of the images had been changed and exclaimed: "Taoism is very much respected. Why should Laozi be seated to the right of Buddha?" He then shifted Laozi's image back to its original position.

As a consequence of the repeated shifting, the two clay sculptures were both damaged. Laozi said to Buddha with a smile: "We were both in perfect condition, but now we have been injured by those two villains."

搬　　像

一庙中塑一老君像在左，塑一佛像在右。有和尚看见，曰："我佛法广大，如何居老君之右？"因将佛搬在老君之左。又有道士看见，曰："我道教极尊，如何居佛之右？"因将老君又搬在佛之左。彼之搬之不已，不觉把两座泥像都搬碎了。老君笑与佛说："我和你两个本是好好的，都被那两个小人搬弄坏了。"

74. A Broken Sedan Chair

In the course of a wedding procession the floor of a bridal sedan chair broke, leaving the bearers in a quandary. Though it was wrong for the bride to walk to the bridegroom's house, it would take too long to fetch another sedan chair to continue the procession. At this moment, the bride broke her silence and said: "I have found a way out. You carry the sedan chair and I will walk inside it."

坠 轿 底

一新嫁者，中途轿底忽坠，轿夫相议，谓："新妇既不可徒行，欲换轿，转去又远。"女闻之曰："我倒有一计。"众喜闻之，答曰："汝外面自抬，我里面自走。"

75. Impetuous Disposition

A man with an impetuous disposition went to a noodle shop and shouted: "Why aren't my noodles ready?" The shop owner came out, slammed a bowl of noodles on the table and said: "Hurry up, I want this bowl emptied."

The customer became indignant at this, and when he got home he told his wife what had happened. He then added: "I'm so angry I want to die." His wife packed up her bags quickly and said: "Since you are dead, I am going to remarry."

A day after the wedding, the bridegroom wanted a divorce for the same reason that she had not given birth to a child.

性　　急

性急人过面店即乱嚷曰："为何不拿面来?"主人持面至，倾之桌上曰："你快吃，我要净碗。"其人怒甚，归谓妻曰："我气死了。"妻忙打包袱曰："你死，我去嫁人。"及嫁过一宿，后夫欲出之归，问故，曰："怪你不养儿子。"

76. At the Cost of a Sound Sleep

Two brothers pooled their money and bought a pair of shoes. The elder brother, however, wore the shoes most of the time. Realizing that he had paid an equal share of the cost but seldom had chance to wear the shoes, the younger brother would put on the shoes and take a walk every night when his brother went to bed.

When the shoes wore out, the elder brother suggested: "Let's pool our money again and buy a new pair." But the younger brother replied: "If we buy a new pair, I'll be sure to lose a lot of sleep."

买　靴

兄弟二人攒钱买了一双靴，其兄常穿之，其弟不肯空出钱，待其兄夜间睡了，却穿上到处行走，遂将靴穿烂。

其兄说："我们将再出钱来买靴。"其弟曰："买靴误了睡。"

77. Born Too Late

Lu Gong lost his wife in old age and married a young woman named Zhu, who was quite upset at the marked difference in their ages. Lu asked her: "Are you unhappy about my age?" She answered: "No."

"Or don't you think that my position is high enough?" Again she answered: "No."

Lu continued: "Then why are you so unhappy?" Zhu said: "Neither your age nor your official rank upsets me. My only grievance is that I was born too late to see your face when you were young."

生　太　晚

卢公暮年丧妻，续弦祝氏，甚少艾。然祝以非偶，每日攒眉。卢见而问曰："汝得非恨我年大耶？"曰："非也。""抑或恨我官卑耶？"曰："非也。"卢曰："然则为何？"祝曰："不恨卢郎年纪大，不恨卢郎官职卑；只恨妾身生太晚，不见卢郎年少时。"

78. A Difference in Speed

Guan Yu had a fine steed that could gallop one thousand *li* in a day. Zhou Cang accompanied him the same distance each day with a big fighting sword in his hand. Guan Yu was eager to obtain a fine steed for Zhou Cang to save him so much physical exertion. Finally a horse was found but it could only cover nine hundred *li* per day. Nevertheless, he bought it for a high price and presented it to Zhou Cang.

Zhou Cang now accompanied Guan Yu on horseback, but their horses differed in the speed they could run. So before he lost sight of Guan Yu, Zhou Cang tied the hooves of his horse together and hung the beast from the handle of his sword. In this way, Zhou Cang would always remain by Guan Yu's side.

千 里 马

关公乘赤兔马，日行千里。周仓握刀从之，日亦千里。公怜之，欲觅一良马赐焉，而遍索无千里者。止一马，日行九百，乃厚价市之赠仓。仓乘马从公，一日差百里，两日差二百里。仓恐失公，仍下马步行，又不忍弃马，乃以索攒马蹄，悬之刀头，掮之而飞走。

79. The Difficulty of Becoming an Immortal

In the past bribery was a common practice in China. A man posing as Lü Dongbin had wrapped up some copper cash and fastened it to the top of his walking stick. When he walked down the street, children pulled on his robe and begged him for money. He gave each of them one cash. Walking a little distance further, a child blocked his path. He too was given one cash. After this went on several more times, the man sighed and said: "If I have to pay for every pace I take, I'll never become an immortal."

Note: Lü Dongbin of the Tang Dynasty was said to have mastered the art of attaining immortality. He was one of the famous eight immortals.

神 仙 难 做

时俗贿赂公行，上下沿习。一人作吕纯阳状，杖头挑钱百文，众小儿牵衣乞钱，即与一文，行未一步，又一儿牵袂以乞，又与一文，才移足，儿又乞钱，如是者，三四不止。纯阳抚掌叹曰："步步要钱，教我神仙也难做。"

80. Two Gestures for the Same Purpose

Zhang Xuzi boasted of having a fine bed. But as it stood in his bedroom, no outsider could see it. Thus he pretended to be sick to enable his relatives and friends to see him in it. You Yangzi, a relative of his, had a pair of new socks which he too wished others to see. So You rolled up his robe and sat with his legs folded.

You asked Zhang what the trouble was. The latter smiled and said: "I have the same trouble as you."

同 病

张诩子缮一榻丽，以在卧内，人未有见，故托病卧榻上，致姻友省问观之。其姻尤扬子者，新制一袜，亦欲章示；其人故搴裳交足加膝而坐，已问曰："君何病？"张诩子睹尤扬子状若是，相视而笑曰："吾病亦若病也。"

81. Sour Cakes

A cake hawker became hoarse, and someone asked him why. He replied: "I'm hungry." The man added: "Why don't you have some of your cakes if you are hungry?" The hawker said: "But they're all spoiled."

糕

有 叫卖糕者，声甚哑。人问其故，曰："我饿耳。"问："既饿，何不食糕？"曰："是馊的。"

82. An Idiot

Yu Ren, an old friend of Aizi, had a daughter two years old. Aizi tried to arrange a marriage between his son and Yu Ren's daughter. Yu asked him: "How old is your son?" Aizi replied: "Four years old." Yu Ren said in amazement: "Are you asking my daughter to marry an old man?"

Aizi was puzzled and asked him why. Yu answered: "Your son is four years old, but my daughter is only two. If my daughter marries at twenty, your son will be forty. If the wedding takes place when she is twenty-five, your son will be fifty years old, an old man already!"

Aizi realized Yu's ignorance and broke off the match-making talks then and there.

老　　　配

虞任者，艾子之故人也，有女生二周，艾子为其子求聘。任曰："贤嗣年几何？"答曰："四岁。"任艴然曰："公欲配吾女子老翁邪？"艾子不谕其旨，曰："何哉？"任曰："贤嗣四岁，吾女二岁，是长一半年纪也；若我女二十而嫁，贤嗣年四十，又不幸二十五嫁，则贤嗣五十矣，非嫁一老翁邪？"艾子知其愚而止。

83. Whence All These Tears?

Emperor Shizu of the Song Dynasty said to Liu Deyuan: "If you weep over the death of the imperial concubine you will be rewarded for your sorrow." Liu immediately broke into tears and wailed loudly, beating his chest and stamping his feet. The emperor was pleased with this show of grief and bestowed on him the post of magistrate of Yuzhou Prefecture.

The emperor did the same to the physician Yang Zhi, who likewise wept and displayed deep sorrow at the death of the imperial concubine. A few days later, someone asked Yang: "How did you manage to burst into tears all of a sudden?" His reply was: "I have done this in anticipation of my concubine's death."

此 副 急 泪

宋世祖谓刘德愿曰:"卿哭贵妃, 悲者当厚赏。"德愿应声恸哭, 抚膺擗踊, 涕泗交流。上甚悦, 故用豫州刺史以赏之。上又令医术人羊志哭贵妃, 志亦呜咽极悲。他日有问志者, 曰:"卿那得此副急泪?"志曰:"我尔日自哭亡妾耳。"

84. An Unworthy Son

Prime Minister Jin was from Dantu County. He had an unworthy son, yet his grandson passed the imperial examinations. Every time the old minister reproached his son, the latter would say: ''Your father is not as good as my father, and your son is not as good as my son. How can anyone say I'm unworthy?''

The old man burst into laughter.

靳 阁 老 子

丹徒勒阁老，有子不肖，而其子之子却又登第。阁老每督责之，即应曰：“翁父不如我父，翁子不如我子，我何不肖？”阁老大笑而止。

85. The Antiquarian of Qin

A scholar of the Qin Dynasty was fond of collecting curios and bought them even at high prices. One day, a man appeared before his gate with an old mat and said: ''Duke Ai of the state of Lu presented this mat to Confucius. This is the very mat upon which the sage sat.'' The scholar was deeply impressed and offered him a plot of land in exchange for it.

Several days later, another man arrived with an old walking stick and stated: ''This stick was actually used by King Tai of the Zhou Dynasty when he fled from Bin and was several hundred years older than the mat used by Confucius. What will you offer me for this?'' The scholar bought it with his entire family fortune.

Later, a man came with a broken bowl which he claimed was made by Emperor Jie of the Xia Dynasty, much earlier than the Zhou Dynasty. The scholar was eager to buy this curio and exchanged his residence for it.

The three curios came into his possession at the cost of his land, family fortune and residence. Because of his fondness for antiques, he was reluctant to part with any of them, though at the time he lacked the means of subsistence. So he put Confucius' mat on his back, took the stick of King Tai in his hand and used Emperor Jie's bowl to go begging in the streets. He cried out: ''You who are generous of heart and who possess all the wealth of ancient coins, please donate one cash to me.''

秦 士 好 古

秦朝有一士人，酷好古物，价虽贵必求之。一日，有一人携败席踵门告曰："昔鲁哀公命席以问孔子，此孔子所坐之席。"秦士大惬意，以为古，遂以附郭田易之。逾时，又一人持古杖以售之，曰："此乃太王避狄，策杖去豳时所操之箠也，盖先孔子之席数百年，子何以偿我？"秦士倾家资与之。既而又有人持朽碗一只，曰："席与杖皆未为古，此碗乃桀造，盖商又远于周。"秦士愈以为远，遂虚所居之宅而予之。三器既得，而田资罄尽，无以衣食，然好古之心，终未忍舍三器，于是披哀公之席，把太王之杖，执桀所作之碗，行丐于市曰："衣食父母，有太公九府钱，乞一文！"

181

86. Drying Books in the Sun

Hao Long was lying flat on his back in the sun on the seventh day of the seventh lunar month. When someone asked him what he was doing, he said: "I am drying the books."

Note: The expression "an abdomen full of books" means that one has a deep store of knowledge.

我　晒　书

郝 隆七月七日出日中仰卧，人问何故，答曰："我晒书。"

87. Thoughtful Advice

With a pole in his hands, a man of the state of Lu was about to pass through a city gate. First he held the pole vertically, but since the gate was not very high, he failed to get through. Holding it horizontally, then, he also failed to get through, since the gate was not wide enough. At this point, an old man appeared and offered to remedy the man's quandary. He said: ''I am not a sage, but I have considerable experience. Why not cut the pole into two?''

执 竿 入 城

鲁有长执竿入城门者，初竖执之，不可入，横执之，亦不可入，计无所出。俄有父老至曰："吾非圣人，但见事多矣。何不以锯中截而入。"遂依而截之。

88. A Good Excuse

An itinerant butcher hung his meat on a wall when he entered a public latrine. Someone tried to steal the meat, but the hawker appeared before he could get away with it. Pressed to make up an excuse for his act, the thief placed the meat in his mouth and stood there without moving. He said: "If you hang it on the wall, it is bound to be stolen. It's much safer for me to keep it in my mouth like I am doing."

偷　　肉

甲卖肉，过入都厕，挂肉著外。乙偷之，未得去，甲出觅肉，因诈便口衔肉云："挂著外门，何得不失？若如我衔肉著口，岂有失理？"

89. A Poor Memory

A man from Huxian County in Shaanxi had a poor memory. One day he went out to chop wood with his wife. Leaving his axe on the ground, he walked a distance away to move his bowels. When he stood up, he noticed the axe on the ground and said: "Look, someone's left an axe behind." He was so overjoyed that he jumped up and down, but ended up stepping on his own excrement. He said: "Someone must have moved his bowels here and forgotten his axe."

His wife noticed what her idiotic husband was doing and said: "You brought the axe here to chop wood, but because you relieved yourself you left the axe on the ground. Have you forgotten all of this?"

The man stared at his wife and said: "What's your name, Madam? Haven't I seen you before somewhere?"

鄂 县 人

鄂县有一人多忘，将斧向田斫柴，并妇亦相随。至田中遂急便转，因放斧地上，旁便转记，忽起见斧，大欢喜云："得一斧。"乃作舞跳跃，遂即自踏着大便处，乃云："只应是有人因大便遗却此斧。"其妻见其昏忘，乃语之云："向者君自将斧斫柴，为欲大便，放斧地上，何因遂即忘却？"此人又熟看其妻面，乃云："娘子何姓，不知何处记识此娘子？"

90. A Missed Drink

A man fond of drinking had a dream. He dreamed that some good wine was offered to him and he began to warm it ready to drink. But at this juncture, he suddenly woke up and said to himself with regret: ''I should have drunk the wine without warming it.''

好　饮

—— 好饮者梦得美酒，将热而饮之，忽然梦醒，乃大悔曰：
"恨不冷吃！"

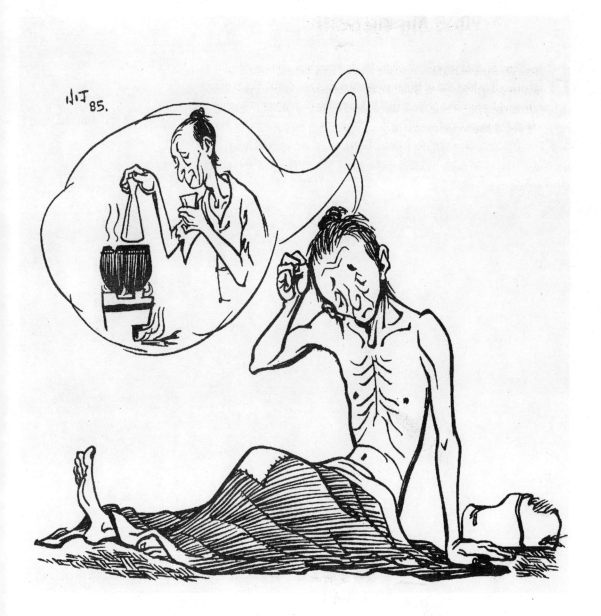

91. Big Eyeballs

Before dinner one night, a man ate a large fish, but served a plate of smaller ones to his guest. Since he was careless, he left the eyes of the large fish on the plate. These were discovered by his guest, who said jokingly: ''I would like to have some of your young fish for breeding.'' The host replied modestly: ''All the fish I keep in my pond are too small for breeding.'' His guest said: ''This must be a rare breed. The fish are small, but they have big eyes.''

大　　　眼

主人自食大鱼，却烹小鱼供宾，误遗大鱼眼珠于盘，为客所觉，因戏言："欲求鱼种，归蓄之池。"主谦曰："此小鱼耳，有何足取。"客曰："鱼虽小，难得这双大眼睛。"

92. Camouflage with Leaves

A poor man from the state of Chu once read the following in a book: "A mantis camouflaged itself while waiting to pounce on a cicada." The man then gathered some leaves from under a tree and used them to camouflage himself. When he asked his wife if she could identify him, she spoke truthfully and said, "Yes, I can." The man then changed his posture and asked her several more times. Becoming annoyed by this practice, she finally told him that she was unable to identify him. The man was very glad.

Thus camouflaged with leaves the man went to the market and stole things from the open stalls. But he was caught and summoned to the magistrate's court. After the man confessed, the magistrate burst into laughter and set him free. He found the man's conduct so inane that he decided not to punish him.

以 叶 隐 形

楚人贫居，读《淮南方》："得螳螂伺蝉自障叶，可以隐形。"遂于树下仰取叶－螳蜋执叶伺蝉－以摘之，叶落树下；树下先有落叶，不能复分别，扫取数斗归，一一以叶自障，问其妻曰："汝见我不？"妻始时恒答言："见。"经日乃厌倦不堪，绐云："不见。"嘿然大喜，赍叶入市，对面取人物，吏遂缚诣县。县官受辞，自说本末，官大笑，放而不治。

93. The Man Who Bit off His Nose

Two men had a quarrel. In the heat of the squabble, one man bit off the nose of the other. Arraigned before the local judge, the first man alleged that the other man had bitten his own nose off. The judge said: "His nose is clearly located above his mouth. How could he possibly bite his own nose off?" The first man replied: "He did it standing on a bench."

啮　鼻

甲与乙斗争，甲啮下乙鼻，官吏欲断之，甲称乙自啮落。

吏曰："夫人鼻高耳，口低岂能啮之乎？"甲曰："他踏床子就啮之。"

94. Distrusting Oneself

A man of the state of Zheng went out to buy a pair of new shoes and measured his feet accordingly, but when he arrived at the market he found that he had forgotten to bring the measurements with him. He picked out a pair of shoes, but was reluctant to buy them. So he left the market and went back home. When he returned the market was closed. Someone said to him: "Why didn't ycu try on the shoes?" He replied: "I place more trust in my ruler than in myself."

郑 人 买 履

郑人有买履者，先自度其足而置之坐，其至市，忘操之也，得履，乃曰："吾忘度。"乃归取之，及反，市罢，不得售。人曰："何不试以足？"曰："宁信度，无自信也。"

95. Hiding a Thief's Coat

One night, a thief sneaked into the house of a poor man, where there was hardly anything to steal. Noticing a large container of rice under the bed, the thief decided to steal it but had nothing to place the rice in. So he took off his coat and spread it on the floor in order to wrap up the rice.

A couple was sleeping in the bed. The husband woke up and saw what the thief was doing in the light of the moon. As the thief busied himself with rice container the husband picked up the thief's coat and hid it in the bedding. Thus when the thief turned to pour the rice out of the container he couldn't find his coat.

At this juncture, the man's wife woke up and said to her husband: ''I hear some strange noises. Perhaps there's a thief in the room.'' The husband said: ''I've been awake for some time now. There's no thief here.''

The thief became rather puzzled when he heard this. He retorted: ''But there must be a thief here somewhere. Somebody has stolen my coat.''

藏 贼 衣

有一贼入人家偷窃，奈其家甚贫，四壁萧然，床头止有米一坛；贼自思将这米偷了去，煮饭也好。因难于携带，遂将自己衣服脱下来，铺在地上，取米坛倾米包携。此时床上夫妻两口，其夫先醒，月光照入屋内，看见贼返身取米时，夫在床上悄悄伸手，将贼衣抽藏床里。贼回身寻衣不见。其妻后醒，慌问夫曰：“房中习习索索地响，恐怕有贼么？”夫曰：“我醒着多时，并没有贼。”这贼听见说话，慌忙高喊道：“我的衣服，才放在地上，就被贼偷了去，怎的还说没贼？”

96. A Golden Birthday Present

An official was making arrangements to celebrate his birthday. His subordinates, knowing that he was born in the Year of the Rat, collected money and bought a gold rat at the goldsmith's shop to mark the occasion. The official was happy to receive this gift and told his subordinates: "My wife's birthday is approaching. She was born in the Year of the Ox."

奶 奶 属 牛

—— 官府生辰，吏曹闻其属鼠，酿黄金铸一鼠为寿。官喜曰："汝知奶奶生辰亦在日下乎? 奶奶是属牛的。"

97. Familial Stubbornness

A father and his son were known for their stubbornness. One day, the father invited a guest for dinner and sent his son to the city to buy some meat. On the way back, the youngster met a man coming in the opposite direction just as they were passing through the city gate. Both of them refused to give way to the other, and they stood there facing each other for a considerable length of time. The father, impatient for the meal to begin, appeared on the scene and told his son: ''Go home with the meat and cook some dishes for my guest. I'll stand here in your place.''

性　　刚

有父子俱性刚不肯让人者。一日，父留客饮，遣子入城市肉。子取肉回，将出城门，值一人对面而来，各不相让，遂挺立良久。父寻至见之，谓子曰："汝姑持肉回陪客饭，待我与他对立在此。"

98. By Force of Habit

On his day off, a cook was preparing a meal at home. While cutting the meat, he stuck a piece of it into his coat pocket. His wife, who was watching him, asked: ''What are you doing? Isn't this our own meat? '' The cook replied: ''But I do this all the time.''

偷 自 家 的 肉

有厨子在家切肉，匿一块于怀中。妻见之，骂曰："这是自家的肉，何为如此？"答曰："我忘了。"

99. Sour Wine

A customer at a wine shop complained that the wine was sour. The shop owner became upset when he heard this and had the customer hung from a beam. Another customer entered the shop and asked what was going on. The shop owner told him: ''The wine on sale at my shop is excellent, but he says it tastes sour. He deserves to be hung from a beam.'' The second customer said: ''Let me have a taste.'' After trying it, he knitted his eyebrows and said: ''Let him go. I'll willingly take his place.''

酸　　酒

有上酒店而嫌其酒酸者，店人怒，吊之于梁。客过问其故，诉曰："小店酒极佳，此人说酸，可是该吊。"客曰："借一杯我尝之。"既尝毕，攒眉谓店主曰："可放此人，吊了我罢。"

100. A Henpecked Husband

A man was beaten by his wife and had little choice but to hide under the bed. His wife screamed at him: ''Come out from there!'' Her husband replied: ''As a real man, I cannot break my word. I shall remain here forever.''

惧　　内

一人被其妻采打，无奈钻在床下。其妻曰："快出来！"其人曰："大丈夫，说不出去定不出去！"

List of Titles

1. Talent in Childhood   12
小时了了

2. Zhuge Ke   14
诸葛恪

3. Deer or River Deer   16
是獐是鹿

4. The Man Who Lost Himself   18
我不见了

5. Six Legs Are Quicker Than Four   20
下公文

6. Reporting a Poor Harvest   22
报荒年

7. Personal Security   24
呆刺史

8. The Ridiculous Magistrate Assistant   26
呆县丞

9. A Man of Phlegmatic Temperament   28
慢性子人

10. The Daughter-in-Law's Glib Tongue   30
巧嘴媳妇

11. A Bargain   32
合做酒

12. The Top Hat 34
    高帽子

13. A Face Painted Red 36
    红脸

14. Wisdom in a Singlc Finger 38
    "一"的妙用

15. Cursive Calligraphy 40
    草字

16. The General's Unworthy Belly 42
    腹负将军

17. No Wine in an Old Bottle 44
    打酒

18. Another Three Catties 46
    再打三斤

19. Yearning for the Third Year 48
    如何熬得到第三年

20. Poor Memory 50
    健忘

21. Neither Salt Nor Vinegar 52
    不吃盐醋

22. A Lost Black Gown 54
    黑色衣服

23. Bargain over a Corpse 56
    尸首买卖

24. Happy Fish 58
    鱼乐

25. A Knock Means No Knock   60
打是不打

26. An Indicator of Age   62
人中主寿

27. An Excessive Ban   64
随身工具

28. A "Bright" Idea Solves a Matrimonial Dilemma   66
如意

29. A Fierce Woman Scares the Emperor   68
帝怕妒妇

30. Choosing A Wife   70
挑选老婆

31. Seven Pairs of Earrings   72
七付耳环

32. Saving a Minister's Life   74
殉　葬

33. Unacceptable Quotations   76
妇人嫉妒

34. Cutting Out the Arrow Shaft   78
剪箭管

35. Playing the Zither in the Street   80
市中弹琴

36. A Soporific   82
瞌睡法

37. Avoiding a Second Fall   84
跌

38. Who Will Look After Me?   86
谁养活我

39. Salted Eggs   88
腌蛋

40. Why Dogs Show No Respect to Beggars   90
狗咬

41. Why People Shiver in Cold Weather   92
冷和抖

42. A Difference of Words   94
三不要

43. Exploiting the Earth   96
剥地皮

44. A Pair of Wild Talkers   98
兄弟虚妄

45. Longing for the Human World   100
仙女思凡

46. Don't Damage the Tiger's Skin   102
莫砍虎皮

47. A New Robe   104
夸新裙

48. Hot Tea   106
热得有趣

49. Buzi and His New Trousers   108
卜子做裤

50. An Unsuccessful Haircut   110
头嫩了

51. Cooking a Goose   112
争雁

52. The Pain Next Door   114
让他去邻家痛

53. A Felt Hat   116
热死我

54. Stealing a Pair of Shoes   118
剌史偷鞋

55. No Difference in Price   120
一靴九百

56. An Empty Abdomen   122
肚里没有

57. Chewing Sugarcane   124
嚼甘蔗渣

58. Talking to a Golden Arhat   126
问金罗汉

59. The Death of a Lazy Woman   128
懒妇

60. The Missing Leg   130
觅凳脚

61. Walking in the Rain   132
徐行雨中

62. A Fart   134
骂放屁

63. Ignorance   136
恍惚

64. Painting the Back of One's Head   138
画行乐

65. How to Get Rich Quick   140
愿换手指

66. Beijing Beating Me Better   142
拳头好得狠

67. Revenge   144
出气

68. A Guest's Witty Remark   146
背客吃饭

69. The Emperor's Crown and Robe   148
皇帝衣帽

70. A Fondness for Drinking   150
好酒

71. Perpetual Drowsiness   152
好睡

72. Tailoring Official Gowns   154
裁缝

73. Moving the Sacred Images   156
搬像

74. A Broken Sedan Chair   158
坠轿底

75. Impetuous Dispositions   160
性急

76. At the Cost of a Sound Sleep   162
买靴

217

77. Born Too Late   164
生太晚

78. A Difference in Speed   166
千里马

79. The Difficulty of Becoming an Immortal   168
神仙难做

80. Two Gestures for the Same Purpose   170
同病

81. Sour Cakes   172
糕

82. An Idiot   174
老配

83. Whence All These Tears?   176
此副急泪

84. An Unworthy Son   178
靳阁老子

85. The Antiquarian of Qin   180
秦士好古

86. Drying Books in the Sun   182
我晒书

87. Thoughtful Advice   184
执竿入城

88. A Good Excuse   186
偷肉

89. A Poor Memory   188
鄠县人

90. A Missed Drink   190
  好饮

91. Big Eyeballs   192
  大眼

92. Camouflage with Leaves   194
  以叶隐形

93. The Man Who Bit off His Nose   196
  啮鼻

94. Distrusting Oneself   198
  郑人买履

95. Hiding a Thief's Coat   200
  藏贼衣

96. A Golden Birthday Present   202
  奶奶属牛

97. Familial Stubbornness   204
  性刚

98. By Force of Habit   206
  偷自家的肉

99. Sour Wine   208
  酸酒

100. A Henpecked Husband   210
  惧内

图书在版编目（CIP）数据

古趣集/丁聪编绘

－北京：新世界出版社，1986（2000.2重印）

ISBN 7－80005－073－4

Ⅰ.古… Ⅱ.丁… Ⅲ.漫画-作品集-中国-现代 Ⅳ.J228.2

中英对照

古　趣　集

丁　聪　编绘

*

新世界出版社出版

（北京百万庄路24号）

新华书店北京发行所发行

北京新华印刷厂印刷

850×1168（毫米）1/24 开本

1986 年第一版　2000 年第六次印刷

ISBN 7-80005-073-4／J·062

定价：24.00 元